CATHOLIC SOCIAL TEACHING IN ACTION

Jesuit Centre for Faith and Justice

Catholic Social Teaching in Action

the columba press

First published in 2005 by
the columba press
55A Spruce Avenue, Stillorgan Industrial Park,
Blackrock, Co Dublin

Cover by Bill Bolger
Origination by The Columba Press
Printed in Ireland by Betaprint, Dublin

ISBN 1 85607 490 0

The Jesuit Centre for Faith and Justice engages in research, social analysis and theological reflection on issues in relation to equity in Irish society, homelessness, young people at risk, international debt and development, refugees and asylum seekers, social spirituality. The Centre also engages in direct work for change by communicating its reflection to policy-making groups and to the general public, and by networking with others to lobby for a more just society and culture.

Copyright © 2005, The Contributors

Table of Contents

Preface   6

Foreword
    Peter McVerry SJ   7

1. A Vision To Live By
    Jim Corkery SJ   11
2. Catholic Social Teaching: The Real 'Third Way'
    David Begg   22
3. The Medellín Document of 1968
    Michael Bingham SJ   33
4. Subsidiarity and the Family
    Finola Kennedy   48
5. Retreat of the Father
    Paul Andrews SJ   58
6. Catholic Social Teaching and *DORAS Luimní*
    Ann Scully RSM   68
7. Action for Justice
    Ronan Barry   77
8. Catholic Social Teaching: Opening the Chest
    Susan Jones CHF   86
9. Subsidiarity, UN-Habitat and Parish Work in Kenya
    Gerard Whelan SJ   103
10. Catholic Social Teaching in Education
    David Tuohy SJ   113
11. Solidarity in Catholic Social Teaching
    Cathy Molloy   128
12. The Social Doctrine for a Christian Practice of Liberation
    Brendan MacPartlin SJ   140

The Contributors   155

Preface

With this collection of articles on the theme of Catholic social teaching the Jesuit Centre for Faith and Justice aims to make more widely known something of what is often referred to as 'the church's best-kept secret'.

The teaching of the church has always been concerned with social matters. For more than a hundred years, beginning with the 1891 Encyclical of Pope Leo XIII, *Rerum Novarum*, *(On the Conditions of Labour)*, issues of justice and peace have been treated in many documents as the popes have responded to social concerns in a changing world.

In *Catholic Social Teaching in Action*, rather than following any chronological order, or set of themes, we simply invited our twelve contributors, from a wide variety of backgrounds, to write briefly about some aspect of the social teaching that has particular significance for them. The intention therefore is not to be comprehensive, nor to suggest that all aspects of the social teaching are touched upon by the authors. What we have are those aspects that have been inspirational in the life and work of the contributors. We hope that if the authors found them to be exciting and challenging then others, who may be discovering them for the first time, might be similarly surprised and challenged in a constructive way.

The Jesuit Centre for Faith and Justice acknowledges with gratitude the generosity of each of the authors in contributing to this project.

Cathy Molloy
Editor

Foreword

Some twenty-five years ago, the Jesuit Centre for Faith and Justice, where I was working with two other colleagues, was asked to give a workshop to a group of Irish clergy on Justice in Irish Society. We decided to divide the workshop into three modules: one on Ireland's economic development, one on social divisions and one on the church's social teaching. We tossed to see who would do what, and the social teaching module fell to me – or on me (at least that's what it felt like). Now I knew absolutely nothing about the church's social teaching (a minor detail which never stopped me talking authoritatively about any subject) and had even less interest in it, so with a groan and a heavy heart, I gathered the relevant documents and a few commentaries and locked myself away for a few dire weeks of study and reflection. To my amazement, I grew very enthused about what I was discovering to be a very rich and radical teaching which had developed over the previous century and which was still developing. When I presented the talk to the assembled group of over 100 priests and quite a few bishops, their unanimous reaction was one of astonishment that, in all their training and ministry, they had never been exposed to this wonderfully relevant and radical thinking at the centre of the church. Such was my first encounter with what has been described as 'the church's best-kept secret'.

While the Roman Catholic Church is often perceived as being very conservative (with much justification), many of the documents which comprise the social teaching of the church came in for much criticism from the dominant power groups in Western society (and indeed within the Catholic Church) at their time, and three have been labelled 'Marxist' by the right-wing press. Some of this teaching would still be very relevant to our world today and still be considered very radical.

Leo XIII's *Rerum Novarum* in 1891 addressed the exploitation of workers by their employers and is just as relevant to the conditions in much of the Majority World today. Its core recommendations, radical in their time – that a just wage is a moral imperative and that workers have the right to join trade unions – are still unheeded in that world and even in parts of our Minority World.

John XXIII's *Mater et Magistra* in 1961 addressed the divisions that existed in our societies and in our world. Our Taoiseach could do worse than bring the Cabinet away for a day's retreat, reflecting on the notion of the common good, developed by John XXIII and on statements such as:

> The economic prosperity of a nation is not so much its total assets in terms of wealth and prosperity, as the equitable division and distribution of this wealth.

Or:

> The utmost vigilance and effort is needed to ensure that social inequalities, so far from increasing, are reduced to a minimum.

On second thoughts, make that a month's retreat.

The Papal Letter, *Justice in the World*, in 1971 produced what is probably the most quoted sentence in church justice documents:

> Action on behalf of justice and participation in the transformation of the world fully appear to us as a constitutive dimension of the preaching of the gospel, or in other words, of the church's mission for the redemption of the human race and its liberation from every oppressive situation.

John Paul II's *On Human Work*, in 1981, with its principle that labour has priority over capital, poses a fundamental challenge to Western capitalism as we know it.

Over the past one hundred and fifteen years, since *Rerum Novarum* was published, the development of the church's social teaching, responding to what Vatican II called 'the signs of the times', although constrained by the circumstances of the day (e.g. the Cold War, which prevented the church from an outright criticism of capitalism at that time) is a fascinating and inspiring story in which Christian values confront issues of the day. Often referred to as a 'Third Way' between capitalism and socialism, the church's social teaching is uncompromisingly critical of both ideologies and their practical implementation in West and East.

In this book, twelve individuals reflect on the significance of this social teaching on their own personal development, on their thinking and in their work. Theologians, educationalists, psychologists, missionaries, parish priests, economists and others share with us what it was in church social teaching that impressed, inspired or helped them in their work for others. From the slums of Nairobi to the education of children in Catholic schools, from the family and role of the father to the training of trade union leaders, to working with refugees, the richness and relevance of the social teaching of the church to the work and thinking of the authors of the articles in this book is described for us.

That the church has failed so often, in many parts of the world, to preach and practice the radical message of liberation which Christ proclaimed, as formulated in this social teaching, is a reflection of the sinfulness of the church and is not a reason to ignore or discard this social teaching as irrelevant. Irrelevant it certainly is not. Challenging it most certainly is. It challenges our comforts, our securities, our set ways of thinking and valuing and acting – if we let it.

It would be my hope that this book might inspire some who, like myself twenty-five years ago, knew little and cared less about the church's social teaching, to begin to explore its invaluable contribution to the development of humankind, its insistence on the fundamental values of the dignity and uniqueness of each individual, and of our need for solidarity with one another, on which is based its critique of the various economic, social and political systems which we have created.

Our world has failed to address seriously the problems of poverty, malnutrition, avoidable illness and premature deaths, which afflict more than a billion of our brothers and sisters, and we are in danger of destroying our own planet in our relentless pursuit of environmentally destructive economic growth. The Catholic Church's social teaching constantly and consistently reminds us of the fundamental challenge which our world forgets at its peril, that 'we are all responsible for all'.

Peter McVerry SJ

CHAPTER ONE

A Vision to Live By

Jim Corkery SJ

For as long as I can remember, I have had a sense that human beings are important. I grew up in the sixties, encountering at an early age the *UN Declaration of Human Rights* and – in religion class at school – documents of the Second Vatican Council such as *Dignitatis Humanae*. I can even say that, from the same early age, I had the wish to do something with my life that would be of benefit to people. Psalm 8 inspired me: 'What is man, that you should keep him in mind, mortal man, that you care for him?' I shared the fascination of my age – late modernity still 'full of itself' – with the greatness of the human being: there was nothing, it seemed, that we would not eventually be able to do; and I wanted to be part of all this doing too. I was only three years old when the Soviets put a man in space. I was fifteen when the US put a man on the moon – and we were able to see him on the television (an invention that had become ubiquitous in the 1960s) talking to President Nixon from there. So I grew up in an era of optimism about human beings and our possibilities; and this imbued me with a sense that I could – and should – make a difference in life myself.

Today, looking back on those heady teenage years, I see what was missing from the vision that was firing me then. And it is thanks, mainly, to Catholic social teaching (CST) that I see the missing elements. Already as a social science student in the mid-1970s I had begun to become aware that what was missing from the vision of my teen years was *a sense of the social*. This awareness was heightened by a decree of the 32nd General Congregation of the Jesuits – I had become a Jesuit student at that stage – arguing that the promotion of justice was integral to the service of faith. So gradually it was dawning on me, through education and experience, that my earlier optic on humanity had been simply too individualistic and that my sense that 'the sky was the limit' for people had to be reconfigured to seeing that it was the limit only for some people – for privileged people, in fact, who enjoyed social circumstances that placed possibilities and opportunities at their fingertips. A document that brought this realisation home to me very strongly was a pastoral letter of the Irish bishops in 1977, which drew on the treasury of Catholic social teaching in a fairly prophetic way to speak about the importance of social justice in the Irish context at that time.

If sociology had already been making me aware that human behaviour was patterned, and not simply a matter of isolated individual actions, now, from this new episcopal document, *The Work of Justice*, I began to realise that the fact that poverty and social deprivation were no accident but part of a pattern, a consequence of how economic and social life were organised in Ireland, meant that, as a young person who publicly professed to be a Christian, I had a responsibility to think much more broadly about humanity than I had been doing. The Letter's insights about how poverty tends to self-perpetuate (Irish Bishops, 1977, 100, 103) alerted me to how people who live in poor areas risk not only 'being branded as poor' but being kept in poverty, not least because their very address lessened their chances of being employed or of obtaining credit. The document pointed out that there was a pattern to the life of the poor, that 'certain identifiable conditions' tended to mark it: ill health, educational deprivation, lack of job skills/training, sub-standard housing. About all these things, the Letter also pointed out, other Irish people did not want to know – just as I, in my earlier and individualistic view of human beings, had not wanted to know about it either and was, indeed, arrested in a way of seeing things that ensured I would not find out.

Inherent Human Dignity, Social Human Nature
My abiding memory from the 1977 Pastoral Letter was its in-

sight that, while it was assumed that poor people lived in ghettos, it went unobserved that the rich did too, because they lived in neighbourhoods that not only blinded them to the plight of less fortunate people, but also prevented them from seeing that it might be incumbent on them to do something about it. Later I found mention of a similar kind of blindness in a poem – I think it was by John Hewitt – that referred to people zooming daily along the tall roads between their salubrious homes well outside Belfast and the financial district of that city without ever touching down among the men and women who bore the heat of the day during all the years of conflict. The poet spoke about them as 'the coasters'; and when I read his words I recalled the economic 'coasters' of *The Work of Justice*. Now here, in practice, was a vision of humanity to which one could not subscribe, for it was a humanity divided. Further contact with CST impressed on me that it was contrary to God's intent for us. Documents of the Second Vatican Council such as *The Church in the Modern World (Gaudium et Spes)*, which is classified by almost every writer on Catholic social teaching as a central text of the Teaching (Schultheis, DeBerri, Henriot, 1987, p 45; also Curran, 2002, p 32), outlawed all discrimination against persons, be it social or cultural, or based on sex, race, colour, social condition, language or religion (see #29). According to Christian tradition, and that document (chapter 1, for example), as well as another key document of Vatican II, *Dignitatis Humanae*, human beings possess a fundamental dignity that must always be acknowledged and respected. This fundamental dignity is, as Pope John Paul only recently reiterated, a transcendent value (John Paul II, 1999, n 2), on the basis of which all men and women are declared equal and must be treated as such. Thus a divided humanity, in which some people had opportunities to flourish while others' basic needs were callously ignored was, in effect, a flouting of Christian faith, indeed a belittling of God's dream for God's people. As such, it constituted, I became aware, a kind of idolatry that was entirely unacceptable.

However, difficulties remained in thinking out a more adequate vision of the human. After all, even in my naïve, teenage vision of humanity I had managed to be aware of each person's dignity. Now, however, I was seeing that an assertion of that dignity without adequate attention to the social conditions needed for its realisation and expression was hollow enough. Equal dignity, after all, meant equal rights; but equal rights were hardly going to be achieved as long as human communities, such as the Irish one, remained divided into ghettos – into 'coasters' and 'coasted-overs'. Thus my emerging vision had to be widened to address what I came to notice, again through CST, as the rights/duties tension; and I saw much more clearly the duties that were incumbent upon people who were the haves – whom today we would refer to as the included – in the community. What I am saying is this: CST's fundamental tenet of equality of dignity meant a vision of human living that took into account both rights and duties, both individual well-being and the common good, both personal flourishing and the development of society as a whole.

The tension that I had become aware of between rights and duties is but one expression of a more fundamental tension that has been identified as lying at the heart of Catholic social teaching (Curran, 2002, pp 131-136): this is the tension between human beings' inalienable personal dignity and fundamentally social nature. In 1999, Pope John Paul II wrote that, because every person is created in God's image and likeness and is therefore radically oriented to relationship, both to relationship with the Creator and with all those created in identical dignity, it can be said that 'to promote the good of the individual is thus to serve the common good, which is that point where rights and duties converge and reinforce one another' (John Paul II, 1999, n 2). This can be stated the other way around as well: to promote the common good is to promote the good of each individual also. For persons and the community are oriented to one another. As human, having been created in love and for love, we are 'persons-in-communities and communities-of-persons'(McDonagh, 1987, p 8).

A Better and More Credible Vision

If at first my contact with CST had the sting of the encounter of King David with the prophet Nathan about it – 'you are the man', the man who has been blind to the true nature of humanity and your true human responsibilities – gradually a sense of freedom emerged with this more communitarian vision of humanity. If at first it seemed that one's obligations were added to hugely, because awareness was growing of how the other half lived – lived, indeed, at the expense of the half to which I was fortunate to belong – it is also the case that a vision was growing that, as human beings who are not isolated 'monads' (Curran, 2002, p. 34), we were not expected to live the moral life on our own but rather *together*, sharing our common task to build a better social life for all. This might have been new to me; but it was not actually new, of course. The notion of the *common good*, which lies at the heart of CST no less than the notion of the individual's inalienable dignity, had a long pedigree. Already before the Second Vatican Council, Pope John XXIII described it as follows: 'The common good is the sum total of all those conditions of social living – economic, political, cultural – which make it possible for women and men to readily and fully achieve the perfection of their humanity. Individual rights are always experienced within the context of promotion of the common good' (John XXIII, 1961).

With the dual 'poles' of individual dignity and common good to the fore, a more credible vision of humanity was now decidedly in place. The twin principles, also central to CST, of subsidiarity and solidarity, which exist to guide Christian action in the shaping of the human world, express the richness of that individual-social tension central to CST, keeping each side ordered to the other and keeping the work of men and women sensitive to the good of both each and all. According to the former principle (subsidiarity), which is particularly mindful of the 'pole' of personal dignity, 'a community of a higher order should not interfere in the internal life of a community of a lower order, depriving the latter of its functions, but rather should support it in case of need and help to co-ordinate its activity with the activities of the rest of society, always with a view to the common good' (John Paul II, 1991, n 48). According to the latter principle (solidarity), which is particularly mindful of the 'pole' of the common good, there is need for 'a firm and persevering determination to commit oneself to the common good; that is to say, to the good of all and of each individual, because we are all really responsible for all' (John Paul II, 1987, n 38). The two principles, as is evident from what has just been written, cannot be stated without reference to one another; and they encapsulate, in action terms, how we are to be respected both as individuals and as members of the human community. Together they put *the truth about humanity that is good and kindly and that is called 'salvation'* into real words.

That last (italicised) statement approximates to a phrase of Cardinal Joseph Ratzinger that I recall him using some years ago. He was making the point that the genuine truth about humanity is salvific truth; it is our salvation. More recently, in a document reflecting on the relationship between men and women, he angered some people by speaking of the church as an 'expert in humanity' (Ratzinger, 2004, p 1), not least because he was claiming such expertise for the church in a context in which many would argue – and not without warrant – that the church still has much progress to make. Yet, insofar as he was speaking in the context of an attempt to acknowledge the equal dignity of men and women and to seek a more full expression of this in human social and ecclesial life, his claim about expertise was not out of place. For the long tradition of Catholic social teaching – and the biblical, patristic, scholastic, theological and praxis-based experience on which it rests (Schultheis et al., 1987, p 9) – can indeed be said to constitute an expertise about humanity, a wisdom about what it is to be and to live humanly that is a valuable map for men and women amid their contemporary struggles to sketch the contours of a more worthwhile social and cultural life and to create a better world for the young people who will follow us. The slogan of a certain political party in

Ireland – 'a lot done, more to do' – is appropriate here; for the teaching recognises that human freedom, being both gift and task, is ever called to a re-receiving of itself as graced gift and to a re-commitment of itself to meet the daily challenges of building a more just world. There is a noble vision of the human here: freed by the grace of God to build relationships between persons and communities; vigilant in that freedom, lest the fragility of these relationships be the cause of their fragmenting. Such vigilance requires a Sisyphus-like determination to keep going, to keep rolling the stones of truth and justice up the steep hill. In short, to persevere with such vigilance requires faith.

A Theological Faith-Vision That Keeps Hope Alive
Catholic social teaching's understanding of humanity has deep roots in theological tradition and is deeply theological itself; it is a faith-vision. Although its wisdom draws much from the fount of natural law reflection and is, in its reasonable character, accessible to all persons of good will, it is also the case that the vision is grounded in strong convictions about the origins, life-journeys and destinies of men and women. Reason and revelation, then, are the sources that enrich it and indeed the foundations upon which it rests. Initially, in my contacts with CST, I found a great dovetailing with my social scientific reflections; later, as a student of theology, I came to see even deeper dimensions. The vision enriched my sense of humanity's dignity because it testified that we were created in love, redeemed by love, and called to eternal love; furthermore, that this love was 'strong as death' and that no flood could quench it (Songs 8: 6-7). And being strong as death, this love instinctively fought for life: for what Pope John Paul II has come to refer to as a 'culture of life,' a culture that values people from cradle to grave – and indeed beyond.

In recent decades, the category of 'culture' has become prominent, not only in postmodern thinking, but also in documents of CST. Already in 1975, Pope Paul VI, in a memorable exhortation seeking to tease out a vision for the renewal of humanity in the final quarter of the twentieth century, argued that 'what matters is to evangelise man's culture and cultures' (Paul VI, 1975, #20). Here was a spelling out of CST in terms recognising that human beings not only shape their cultures but are also shaped by them, so that dialogue between the gospel and a culture is seen to be indispensable if the Christian vision of humanity is to find root in a particular time and place. In a later paragraph of the same document, the Pope talks about evangelisation remaining incomplete if it fails to 'take account of the unceasing interplay of the gospel and of man's concrete life, both personal and social;' and at the end of the paragraph, not surprisingly for that time, he turns to the theme of 'liberation' (Paul VI, 1975, #29). In his treatment of it in subsequent paragraphs (30-39), while he is careful not to identify earthly liberation with the fullness of salvation, he is equally careful to assure his readers of the church's concern for such liberation. There is no explicit reference to liberation theology here, but it is evident that the Pope had both its gifts and its potential excesses in mind. And the presence of liberation theology in his mind may well be one of the influences lending such a radical character to his own document. At the time it was written liberation theology was engaged in the task of radically re-thinking the traditional areas of theology from the perspective of the poor and through a social rather than individual lens, and in so doing it changed dramatically how sin, grace, church, sacraments, Trinity – and God's kingdom or 'dream' for God's beloved humanity – were to be conceived. It noted that theological reflection on sin required an examination of context as well as personal conscience; that grace was poured out on individuals for communities and, indeed, on communities themselves, to bind them together; that the celebration of the eucharist was a sham if the discriminations outlawed in *Gaudium et spes* (n 29) were practised; that the 'new heaven and new earth' of Christian eschatology (see Rev 21:1) was not a 'pie-in-the-sky' daydream to distract Christians from human suffering but rather to commit them to the alleviation of it on this present earth; and that the Three-Personed God, communion itself, was asking that we, who are created in the divine image, might live in communion also. All these viewpoints were permeating the theological atmosphere of the time and, for all its careful distinguishing of socio-political from eschatological liberation, it can be argued that the radical character of Paul VI's own document owed something to the liberation theology that was flourishing at the time when he was writing.

What had opened up here through all this social-theological reflection was a vision, a vision to live by, a vision centred on what, in theology, was known as an anthropology. In a recent work on CST, the eminent moral theologian Charles E. Curran pointed to the centrality of anthropology, an understanding of humanity, for the teaching. Even though it had not developed a systematic social ethics, Curran noted, it had recognised 'the fundamental importance of anthropology as the basis for its teaching' (Curran, 2002, p 127). When reflecting recently on one hundred years of social teaching, Pope John Paul II had observed (Curran said) that the human person is the principle inspiring the church's social doctrine (John Paul II, 1991, n 11). This is a point that was present in *Quadragesimo Anno* (1931, n 42), added Curran, and indeed in *Gaudium et spes* at the second Vatican Council (1965) also, the whole structure of which document 'shows that anthropology is the key to understanding Catholic social teaching' (Curran, 2002, p 128). Grasping this centrality of anthropology excited me when I first encountered Catholic social teaching and it still excites me today – even if the anthropology will always require updating. Indeed it will require it even from beyond its own boundaries as it seeks to grapple with matters of vital importance today: cultures, care of the earth, relationships of men and women, technology, globalisation. But it is well placed to grapple with these things because it rests on an anthropology at once sturdy, as regards core vision, yet flexible, as regards its application to the concrete problems that arise in our ever-changing circumstances.

And yet: how dare I wax lyrical about a vision, when there remain so many problems staring us in the face? Here a remark of the late Henri Nouwen comes to mind, who once said, with regard to liberation theology, that it should have provided itself with a spirituality of failure. Is not the same true of Catholic social teaching, the practitioners of which (as was said already) require a sustained, dogged, Sisyphus-like, stone-pushing commitment to stay at their task? Yes. But – and this is the case precisely and only with a vision that is centred not exclusively on an earthly utopia and that does not gauge all of its success by definable 'measurables' – continued commitment is possible when one remains aware of one's penultimate status in bringing about the better future, as well as of one's inability – and, since it belongs to our humanity, one's not needing – to see the whole picture. You may laugh at Jimmy Stewart in that celebrated movie, *It's a Wonderful Life*; or, indeed, at the apparently unrealistic father in the more recent film, *La Vita e Bella*. But what these two 'fools' testify to, in their very different ways, is that hope-against-hope is not groundless, if one grasps the webbed – indeed the almost 'infectious' – character of goodness and if one's own ultimate motivation is love. What undergirds CST's vision of the human is God's vision of the human: transcendent, social, and, as far as God's own heart is concerned, the object of an inexhaustible love, a love for which the Son of God went to his death and, in that death, proved love to be the stronger. So there is at least a spirituality for failure here, a spirituality rooted in a praxis that will never give up because, while on the one hand it is ruggedly incarnational and earthed, on the other hand it is enlivened by the assurance that there is something stronger than death here.

Bibliography

Curran, Charles E., *Catholic Social Teaching: A Historical, Theological, and Ethical Analysis*. Washington DC: Georgetown University Press, 2002.

Irish Bishops' Pastoral, *The Work of Justice*. Dublin: Veritas Publications, 1977.

Pope John XXIII, Encyclical Letter *Mater et Magistra*. London: Catholic Truth Society, 1963 (issued 15 May, 1961).

Pope John Paul II, Encyclical Letter *Centesimus Annus*. 1991.

Pope John Paul II, Encyclical Letter *Sollicitudo Rei Socialis*. 1987.

Pope John Paul II, World Day of Peace Message. 1999.

McDonagh, Enda, *The Gracing of Society*. Dublin: Gill and Macmillan, 1987.

Pope Paul VI, Apostolic Exhortation *Evangelii Nuntiandi*. London: Catholic Truth Society, 1975 (issued 8 December 1975).

Pope Pius XI, *Quadragesimo Anno*. 1931.

Ratzinger, Joseph Cardinal (as Prefect of the Congregation for the Doctrine of the Faith), *Letter to the Bishops of the Catholic Church on the Collaboration of Men and Women in the Church and in the World*. Rome: May 31, 2004. Available on the web at www.zenit.org/english/visualizza.phtml?sid=57636

Second Vatican Council, Pastoral Constitution on the Church in the Modern World *Gaudium et Spes*, in: Austin Flannery OP (ed.). *Vatican Council II: The Conciliar and Post Conciliar Documents*. Dublin: Dominican Publications, 1975, pp 903-1001 (issued 7 December, 1965).

Schultheis, Michael J; DeBerri, Edward P; Henriot, Peter J., *Our Best Kept Secret: The Rich Heritage of Catholic Social Teaching*. Revised, Expanded Edition. Washington DC: Centre of Concern, 1987.

CHAPTER TWO

Catholic Social Teaching: The Real 'Third Way'

David Begg

Some years ago, early on a Sunday morning, I was travelling to speak at a conference in Clare and, while listening to a programme on BBC Radio 4, I heard a very interesting perspective on the current relevance of Catholic social teaching. The subject of the programme was an interview with the author Paul Vallely about a book entitled *The New Politics – Catholic Social Teaching for the Twenty-first Century*, which he edited. At that time Bill Clinton and Tony Blair were pushing the concept of 'The Third Way' as a *via media* between free market capitalism and socialism. Anthony Giddons is the author most associated with this idea and Tony Blair in particular seemed very enamoured of it. In the course of the interview Vallely observed that 'if Tony Blair is really interested in exploring a Third Way concept he should speak to his wife Cherie because, as a Catholic, she would know that Catholic social teaching amounts to a comprehensive body of material on this theme'. In other words, the Third Way is already embodied in the sixteen papal encyclicals issued between 1891 and 1995.

There has always been, ever since the Middle Ages, the idea of the just wage, which the Catholic church supported – and which it continues to support as the recent papal encyclical *Evangelium Vitae* (1995) makes clear. When Catholic societies embarked on capitalism in the nineteenth century they tried to retain the idea of the just wage for the worker, and with it notions of the just price, just profit and even the just enterprise. They still do, and it's the reason Christian democratic parties in mainland Europe are as attached as they are to less raw, more stakeholder-oriented capitalism.

It is also true of course that the church, despite the lifestyle of its itinerant founder, had sometimes instinctively taken the side of authority and the rich. And yet it has also always set its face against individualism and defined Christians as persons living in community. Pope Leo XIII set about resolving these contradictory elements.

The result was *Rerum Novarum* (1891), the first in what were to prove a series of papal encyclicals on social issues. When this treatise on the rights of the worker was published it caused shockwaves with its condemnation of a situation in which a 'tiny group of extravagantly rich men have been able to lay upon the great multitude of unpropertied workers a yoke little better than that of slavery itself'. The excesses of capitalism were condemned: 'The first task is to save the wretched workers from the brutality of those who make use of human beings as mere instruments for the unrestrained acquisition of profits.' The medieval notion of a just wage was restated: 'The wage ought not to be in any way insufficient for the bodily needs of a temperate and well-behaved worker. If having no alternative and fearing a worse fate, a workman is forced to accept harder conditions imposed by an employer or contractor, he is the victim of violence against which justice cries out.' Yet for all the vigour of its language – and the fact that it was condemned as a socialist document at the time – it was essentially a plea to the common sense of the ruling classes: 'The condition of the workers is the question of the hour. It will be answered one way or another, rationally or irrationally, and which way it goes is of the greatest importance to the state.'

The key fact was this: in the course of his attempt to shame the rich into better behaviour, the Pope began the process of formulating the set of principles which evolved over the intervening hundred years. Out of this there began to emerge certain core principles. At their heart is the notion of the 'common good' which had its roots in the thinking of the great mediaeval theologian St Thomas Aquinas, who synthesised the thought of Aristotle and St Augustine, bringing together the two great traditions of Western culture – the philosophy of the great classical pagan writers with the theology of the early church fathers. Individualism, leading to both social and economic liberalism, and forms of doctrinaire state socialism, arguably represent two great heresies from the Christian tradition of balancing individual and societal considerations.

In the economic sphere during the twentieth century, this polarisation took the form of one between liberal capitalism on the one hand and socialism on the other. Eventually, however, such extreme polarisation was rejected by a huge majority in most countries. Instead, social democrats now accept the market system but are concerned to modify its operation in such a way as to ensure a more equitable distribution of the fruits of the capitalist system than would emerge if that system were left to itself. By contrast, economic liberals, whilst not in principle opposing some social provision for the disadvantaged, prefer to let market forces prevail as far as possible, and resist pressures to ensure a more equitable spread of resources through state action.

It is important not to understate the differences between both outlooks. The liberal philosophy was enormously boosted by the collapse of the Soviet Union because those, like Francis Fukuyama, who believe in it, saw the end of Communism, wrongly in my view, as an automatic endorsement of free market capitalism.

There is a powerful struggle taking place for the soul of Europe between those who would want it to be no more than a shallow common market and those who want even closer political integration with a view to preserving a social model based substantially on the precepts of solidarity inherent also in Catholic social teaching.

It is true, as a recent article in *The Economist* pointed out, that 'many of the moving spirits of post-war European integration – Konrad Adenauer, Jacques Delors, Alcide de Gasperi and Robert Schuman – were devout Catholics. Their faith gave them a strong sense of the cultural and religious ties between Europeans that transcend national boundaries. The European flag of 12 yellow stars on a blue background also owes something to Catholicism. Arsene Heitz, who designed it in 1955, recently told *Lourdes* magazine that his inspiration had been the reference to the Book of Revelation, the New Testament's final section, to 'a woman clothed with the sun ... and a crown of twelve stars on her head'.

Given this background, it is a little ironic that Catholicism and the European ideal have been in conflict recently. The opposition of the European Parliament to the nomination of Rocco Buttiglione as Commissioner because of his Catholic and conservative values was interesting. The fact, of course, is that Mr Buttiglione's strong views are in the sphere of sexual morality and probably a majority of Catholics (if not the Pope) would disagree with him. Nevertheless, the incident may have been, as *The Economist* argues 'an expression of the tension between secular and religious views of 'European Values' that has been building for some time'.

If one steps aside from the emotional dimension of morality in a narrow sexual context, and the principle of whether God should be mentioned in the constitution, the fact is that Europe as a political entity is still moving in the direction of Catholic social teaching. The new constitution, even if it does not mention God, in the Charter of Fundamental Rights is very much in line with Catholic social teaching. To be sure there are questions of degree involved. The French socialists, for example, divided on whether or not to support the new constitution. The faction led by Mr Fabius argued against it on the grounds that failure to include tax harmonisation would prevent the achievement of socialism. Much to the relief of the European political establishment, the socialists eventually decided to support the constitution. Mr Fabius was probably right about its limitations, yet it is arguably the most progressive document of its kind with the potential to give a level of protection to 450 million citizens, which is formidable. Notwithstanding recent tensions associated with the Buttiglione affair and the reaction to it by the Vatican, the new constitution owes a lot to the influence of Catholic social teaching especially in the context of the post war settlement in Europe. The German social market economy was created after the war as a deliberate break with conservatism, and there is a powerful liberal tradition in German Catholicism. It would be going too far to attribute the full development of Social Europe to Catholic social teaching because to do so would be to understate the influence of the Scandinavian countries, which are predominantly Lutheran, and of course the Dutch and even the secular humanist contribution. But it cannot be denied that its influence has been substantial.

Europe has so far eschewed the buccaneering turbo capitalism emanating from America. What Americans believe is that capitalism is opportunity for all and risk for all – if you win that game you get lucky. It is the alternative tradition of Catholic capitalism, social market capitalism, or stakeholder capitalism – call it what you like – that holds out any hope for social justice in the world. Unfortunately, the US variant is overall in the ascent as globalisation becomes more pervasive. While Europe may be able to stand out against it, the fact is that the developing world presently has no such prospect.

In *The Lexus and the Olive Tree*, Thomas Friedman likens the US to a petrol station in which the petrol is cheap but the customer must serve himself – contrasting that with other parts of the world, where either the petrol is expensive but served to you, or cheap but unavailable because it has been sold on the black market. 'What is going on,' he writes, 'is that through the process of globalisation everyone is being forced towards America's gas station. If you are not American and don't know how to pump your own gas, I suggest you learn ... in so many ways, globalisation is us. We are not the tiger. Globalisation is the tiger. But we are the people most adept at riding the tiger and now we're telling everyone else to get on or get out of the way.'

The outlook for the developing world is dismal. Consider the statistics of global poverty:
- One in six children is severally hungry

THE REAL 'THIRD WAY'

- 800 million people are short of food
- 1.2 billion people live on less than a dollar a day
- 180 million children work in the worst form of child labour
- 1.2 million children are trafficked each year

It is acknowledged now that it will be difficult to meet the UN millennium development goals, such that in ten years time the world will still be a pretty awful place.

While previous encyclicals had inevitably been written from a pre-dominant European perspective, *Populorum Progressio* (1967) attempts to be truly Catholic and planetary. In looking at relations between rich and poor, powerful and powerless, *Populorum Progressio* does at global level what *Rerum Novarum* did at the national. It reflects the thinking of the Dominican priest and economist Louis Lebret, who had been summoned by Pope Paul to be a *peritus* (theological consultant) at the Council and who had been a great help on his mission to the UN in New York to appeal for peace. *Populorum Progressio* made a great impact. François Perroux, Professor at the College de France, regarded it as 'one of the greatest texts of human history' – a profound and original synthesis of the Ten Commandments, the gospel teaching and the Declaration of Human Rights. On the other hand the *Wall Street Journal* regarded *Populorum Progressio* as 'warmed-over Marxism' since it rejected the 'trickle down' theory of development which leaves everything to market forces and assumes that some part of the benefits reaped by the rich will eventually trickle down to the poor. Paul VI particularly incensed the free marketers when he asserted:

> We must repeat once more that the superfluous wealth of rich countries should be placed at the disposal of the poor nations ... Besides, the rich world will be the first to benefit as a result. Otherwise their continued greed will certainly call down on them the judgement of God and the wrath of the poor, with consequences no one can foretell.

Populorum Progressio criticises capitalism more strongly than earlier Catholic social teaching – including in its critique the profit motive and the unrestricted use of private property. Paul VI's support for land reform was audacious and hit a raw nerve in Latin America, where so much land is concentrated in very few hands and where expropriation was (and in some cases still is) regarded as pure and unadulterated Leninism. Equally significant were his discussions of the restriction of capital flows and of industrialisation.

What *Populorum Progressio* has to say about free trade is highly relevant today when the market has been transformed into an idol and we have trade which is neither free nor fair.

It is not that Paul VI has a specific 'Catholic answer' to social and economic problems. What he condemns are the injustices perpetrated by unjust capitalistic trading and he asserts that a just economic order cannot be built on liberal capitalism. He proposes instead the guiding principles of solidarity between rich and poor and of dialogue leading to planning on a global scale. Was this a pipe dream or can anything at all be done to alter the structures of injustice in the world? Well perhaps. If European political integration ever becomes a reality it may have the potential to be an alternative pole of influence in the western world – alternative that is to the United States. If the European value system continues to reflect Catholic social teaching then it will follow this route. Already the EU is the largest donor in terms of international aid. In short, Europe is the hope of the world.

Ireland has followed a somewhat different path from that through which continental Europe has evolved. The first sixty odd years of its existence since the foundation of the state was based on a broad Catholic polity. As such Ireland never had separate Catholic organisations like trade unions in the manner common to other European countries. It was accepted that all elements of civil society would operate on an essentially Catholic ethos. Also, of course, large parts of the education and health infrastructure were, and still are, run by the Catholic Church. Thus Ireland never developed a welfare state in the classic European sense. We have what has been described as 'a mixed economy of welfare'.

The fact that our country for such a long period was constructed on a confessional policy makes it difficult to be objective about the influence of Catholic social teaching. The fact is that it influenced every part of our lives but not always in a benign way. Retrospective evaluation frankly makes some aspects look pretty awful but it didn't necessarily seem so at the time.

The most controversial manifestation of the Catholic social teaching being imposed on the population was the 1951 Mother and Child Scheme. Although in one sense it ruined Dr Noel Browne politically, in another it never diminished him in the eyes of the people. He could have been elected in any constituency in Ireland, which is quite something for a left wing politician.

The two pillars of Catholic social teaching are solidarity – the notion that we are all responsible in some way for one another – and subsidiarity – the ideal that political and social decisions should be taken at the lowest level possible, consonant with good government. These two principles are always in some sense in tension, perhaps in dialectical tension. The East-West conflict and the threat of totalitarian communist regimes had brought to Catholic social teaching a particular emphasis on the subsidiarity side of the equation here in Ireland. Why it should have been so is hard to fathom – perhaps it was our links with America – but it was, and it stunted social development in Ireland.

In the earlier part of this article I argued that Catholic social teaching had a major influence on the European Union. It is slightly ironic that most social policy development in Ireland in the last thirty years was driven by the European Union. It is a measure of the extent to which the domestic interpretation of that teaching was out of line with mainstream European Catholic opinion.

As Garret Fitzgerald put it in his book, *Reflections on the Irish State*:

> The traditional concern of Roman Catholic teaching with excessive emphasis on individualism has in many ways been a

very constructive force in the world. But in the context of the Irish Constitution this concern can be argued to have led in practice to a new imbalance in the other direction, that is to a situation in which the right to property is given a higher value than the right to personal liberty, and in which the ultimate right of the family (defined in a very specific and exclusive way as the family based on marriage), is given a priority over the rights of children. That is a priority which, as the Referendum decision of 1972 showed, the vast majority of our people consider in one respect at least to be unacceptable.

The legacy effect of this narrow interpretation of Catholic social teaching has, in my opinion, been damaging to the church. It spawned a generation of people who resented it deeply and are today fierce critics of the church. While the child abuse scandals have been utterly appalling, the self-inflicted damage has been exacerbated by a public commentary, much of which has been hostile to the church as an institution.

But as the waters of this period subside a new kind of church is emerging, one in which the emphasis on social teaching is very much on the solidaristic pillar. Organisations such as CORI Justice and Peace Office have been very forceful in putting the public case for social justice at home, while Trócaire has advocated for it in the developing world. These organisations are not on their own. Many religious bodies pursue a similar agenda and the hierarchy itself, with its many commissions, has been a consistent and fearless critic of government policy.

Ireland faces many challenges in the sphere of social policy. In one sense we have achieved our economic objectives. Our economy has the lowest unemployment and fastest growth in Europe. We have subordinated everything to this objective but it is time to rebalance the equation. We have many deficits in social provision, most notably in:
- Health Care
- Child Care
- Care of the elderly and people with disabilities

- Housing
- Educational disadvantage

Some of these will be exacerbated by changing demography. The voracious economic machine demands increased labour supply but cares nothing for the cost in terms of caring. Many parents find child care a huge problem and as our elderly population grows and lives longer they will become more frail and in greater need of a proper infrastructure of caring. The collapse of stock market values in the last few years wiped billions of euros off the value of occupational pension schemes such that many people are sleepwalking towards an impoverished old age. These are challenging issues about which there is little or no public discourse. Not enough attention has been given to the problem of reconciling ideological pressure for lower taxation – some of which we have imported from the US – with the exceptional social and infrastructural deficiencies of what was until recently a very poor country by Northern European standards.

In the introduction to *The New Politics* Paul Vallely argues that:

> The political problem of mankind is to combine three things – economic efficiency, social justice and individual liberty – and the modern age has lost the correct balance between the three elements of this political equation.

On the first of these, *Evangelium Vitae* (1995) says that human needs are being sacrificed to the interests of economic efficiency. Man is being reduced to *homo oeconomicus* with all progress judged mainly in terms of economic growth. An excessive emphasis upon efficiency has led to a culture in which others are considered not for what they 'are' but for that they 'have, do and produce'. 'The criterion of personal dignity – which demands respect, generosity and service, is being replaced by the criterion of efficiency, functionality and usefulness' says *Evangelium Vitae*. 'This is the supremacy of the strong over the weak.'

We in Ireland are seriously at risk off falling into this trap. We are pursuing an economic policy of growth at all costs and regardless of the pressure it is putting on our social infrastructure. Full employment is an important instrument for achieving social justice. It is a necessary condition but not enough. Our history of unemployment means that the mantra of economic growth is very congenial to us but we need to start realising its limitations.

The time is opportune for Ireland to decide what sort of country it wants to be. It is very difficult to do so without locating our discourse in some accepted set of values.

I agree with Vallely that Catholic social teaching is the most viable 'Third Way'. Let us hope that there is still a willingness amongst our people to give it a hearing. The forthcoming referendum on the new constitution may be an opportunity to test the waters. Progressive Catholics should not leave the field to the fundamentalist right. We have a good message and we have a responsibility to go out and proclaim it.

Bibliography

Garret FitzGerald, *Reflections on the Irish State: Ireland Since Independence*, Dublin: Academic Press, 2003.

Thomas Friedian, *The Lexus and the Olive Tree*, New York: Farrar, Straus and Giroux, 1999.

Charlemagne, *'The Economist'*, 30 October 2004. 'Real Politics at Last'.

The Guardian, 10 December 2004, 'The Greatest Catastrophe'.

Financial Times, 13/14 November 2004, 'God Has Yet To Leave Europe'.

Paul Vallely (Editor), *The New Politics – Catholic Social Teaching for the Twenty-first Century'*, SCM Canterbury Press, 1998.

Will Hutton and Anthony Giddens (Editors), *On the Edge*, London: Jonathan Cape. 2000.

Will Hutton, *The State We're In*, London: Vintage Books, 1996.

Will Hutton, *The World We're In*, Little, Brown, 2002.

CHAPTER THREE

The Medellín Document of 1968

Michael Bingham SJ

I

It was at a student party in Oxford in 1967, I remember, that I told someone I was training to be a priest. He remarked that as far as he was concerned the church had always and everywhere shown itself to be against human progress and freedom. I was mortified – perhaps because I feared in my heart of hearts that it was true. He cited Latin America where the church, allied to the ruling classes, helped to keep the poor masses in subjection. Had I, I wondered, dedicated my life to such an irrelevant and anti-historical enterprise?

The doubts and questions raised by this casual encounter gnawed away inside me for the next few years. I hadn't yet heard of Camilo Torres, the priest who joined the revolutionary 'National Liberation Army' in Colombia who had been killed in an army ambush only the previous year. Nor, apparently, had my student friend. Still less did I imagine that eight years later I would find myself in Camilo's homeland itself, searching for the answer to that same devastating doubt – but confident now that I was on the right track.

My way there, however, passed through theological training in Canada. Rumours from Latin America of a revolutionary reading of the gospel were already strong here, and the slim volume of Conclusions from the Second General Conference of Latin American Bishops of a few years ago had acquired an almost clandestine status. This Conference, held in Medellín, Colombia, in 1968, was spearheaded by a remarkable group of bishops and theologians who had been inspired by the opening up of the Catholic Church to the modern world with the Second Vatican Council.

Subtitled 'The Church in the Present-Day Transformation of Latin America in the Light of the Council', these Conclusions comprised three documents on 'Peace', 'Justice' and 'Poverty', prefaced by a 'Message to the Peoples of Latin America'.[1] In fact, much of the teaching and statements here through which the Latin American church leaders aimed to address the situation of their own continent, in its political, social and cultural context, were framed in the uncontroversial terms of development theory that underpinned many of the Vatican Council's own forward-looking documents. In other words, that the poverty and injustice that characterised the lives of the vast majority were due to unequal development, or lack of it, and that the solution lay in the channelling of adequate resources from rich nations and classes to poor. But throughout the text there constantly leapt out concepts and ideas that seemed to belong to another language and analysis.

From the very start the bishops interpreted the 'aspirations and clamours of Latin America' as 'signs of the times' revealing a plan of God, and declared their wish to 'feel the problems, perceive the demands, share the agonies, discover the ways and co-operate in the solutions.'[2] They captured the urgency of the moment: 'We are on the threshold of a new epoch in the history of our continent ... a time full of zeal for full emancipation, of liberation from every form of servitude' and spoke of a 'force, daily more insistent and impatient for transformation.'[3]

The 'misery that besets large masses of human beings' in their countries, frustrated in their legitimate aspirations was, they claimed, of vital moral concern – 'an injustice which cries to the heavens.'[4] It was, indeed, what they termed 'institution-

---

1. Second General Conference of Latin American Bishops 'The Church in the Present-Day Transformation of Latin America in the Light of the Council' (August 26–September 6, 1968), in *Liberation Theology: A Documentary History*, ed. Alfred T. Hennelly SJ, Orbis Books, New York, 1990.
2. Ibid, Message to the Peoples of Latin America, p 91.
3. Ibid, Introduction to the Final Documents, 4, p 95.
4. Ibid, Document on Justice, 1, p 97.

alised violence', where what may appear as 'peace and order' is in reality 'nothing but the seed of rebellion and war'.[5] They applied the powerful biblical paradigm of the Exodus of the people of Israel from oppression to interpret the historical process the continent had embarked on from less to more human conditions.[6] Indeed, God's Son was sent to liberate all 'from the slavery to which sin has subjected them', including those 'serious sins evident in unjust structures': 'hunger, misery, oppression and ignorance'.[7] For human improvement and progress, and the better ordering of society, they maintained, were integral to God's design for the world, and of 'vital concern to the kingdom of God'.[8]

As pastors, moreover, they declared they 'cannot remain indifferent to the deafening cry that pours from the throats of millions of men and women', asking them for 'a liberation that reaches them from nowhere else.'[9] From now on, they asserted, it would be the duty of the church to 'awaken an awareness of justice ... defend the rights of the poor and oppressed ... denounce excessive inequalities' between poor and rich, weak and powerful.[10] Enough of reflection, they said – now was the time for action. Within the church itself they would search for a 'new and more dynamic presence.'[11] To 'awaken the social conscience' would form an indispensable part of their pastoral action, encouraging people, especially the poor, to develop 'small basic communities' in order to balance those minority groups in power, and to participate in political life and in the construction of a new society.'[12] They pledged themselves, too, to creating a church that lives in solidarity with the poor, affirming 'the value

---

5. Ibid, Document on Peace, 14, p 109.
6. Ibid, Introduction, 6, p 96.
7. Ibid, Document on Justice, 2 & 3, p 98.
8. Ibid, Document on Justice, 5, p 99.
9. Ibid, Document on Poverty, 1 & 2, p 114.
10. Ibid, Document on Peace, 20-23, p 112.
11. Ibid, Introduction, 8, p 97.
12. Ibid, Document on Justice, 7, 16, 17, 20, pp 100, 103-4.

of the poor in the eyes of God', and exhibiting in its lifestyle a simplicity and material detachment as institutional and personal testimony.[13]

Surely here was a message, I thought, that was radical – one, maybe, of which my Oxford acquaintance might have approved. This presented a challenge, an urgent appeal to join a cause that seemed to make sense of history, of the world, and of faith all at the same time. It was not hard to hear echoes of Jesus' call to the building of the kingdom. I made up my mind that I wanted to be part of the enterprise. Other key texts, such as Gustavo Gutiérrez' seminal *A Theology of Liberation*, were consumed by me with perhaps more enthusiasm than understanding. But two untheological experiences prepared me better than all of this for what was to come.

II

The first of these was some contact with the world of the American Indian through visits to the Jesuit missions in Northern Ontario. Here were the forlorn remains of a culture that had the vestiges – not to say the seeds – of an alternative way of life, of being and relating, of organising society. I recall the sensation of getting down from the ice-bound train one Christmas and approaching the township almost on tiptoe through the snow for fear of damaging fragile sensibilities with my clumsy mental and cultural baggage.

The second experience was as prison chaplain in a women's gaol in the city. Hearing the stories of the inmates – recipients, often, of abuse as much as perpetrators – I found myself looking at the underside of society and discovering that it looked, and felt, completely different. They belonged to the losing side in the game of life, whose odds were stacked against them. I never looked at things in quite the same way ever again. I mention these two valuable insights I was served with here – a sense of respectful presence before the poor, and of seeing the world from the bottom side up – because they were consolidated for

---

13. Ibid, Document on Poverty, 7, 10, 12, pp 116-7.

THE MEDELLIN DOCUMENT

me during my 10 years subsequent sojourn in Latin America, and they have stayed with me ever since.

The close of 1975 found me, eventually, doing my 'tertianship' (or last year of Jesuit training) with a dozen others in a cramped little house in the 'misery belt' of Medellín, Colombia, venue of that famous meeting just seven years earlier. It was in at the deep end, and we threw ourselves into our surroundings. And yet I recall most vividly the contradictions and dilemmas posed by our 'parachuting' into the lives of these chosen neighbours around us, representatives of that vast sub-class of humanity but now become our privileged object of concern.

I felt again the sense of awe, of hesitancy before the vulnerable existences and relationships disturbed or overwhelmed by our appearance. Our professed 'poverty' was a sham in the midst of the humble yet dignified people, for we were by any definition 'rich': rich in money, resources, power, influence, education and opportunities. Yet so poor did we discover ourselves when compared to them in terms of generosity, availability, mutual dependence, authenticity and spontaneity.

Could we – should we – put this 'wealth' of ours at our neighbours' service? If not, how was our plea of wanting to break the pattern of 'paternalism' to be understood? Yet if relationships of power were to be altered and the poor to be agents of their own lives and destiny, then perhaps – so we reasoned – the best gift we could offer them would be to begin to accompany them in their pains and trials, encourage them in their hopes and struggles.

Thus we debated whether we should accept the invitation to be put up for election to the 'Communal Action', or Board of the neighbourhood organisation, and concluded that such a role would only serve to perpetuate the people's sense of impotence and incompetence. It felt, in a real sense, like a 'handing over' – or even 'handing back' – of power and dignity to those to whom it had rightfully belonged, and from whom it had been kept for so long.

It seemed consistent, therefore, when a group of people carried out an illegal 'invasion' of an idle plot of land on the outskirts of the estate and came to ask for support. Their hastily erected shacks of poles and plastic were toppled by the police sent in by the owner, but stubborn rebuilding and resistance eventually won the day. That, after all, was the familiar history of the growth of shanty towns. And wasn't this but another instance of how the law protects the 'haves' and prejudices the 'have nots'? Nor was this 'lawlessness', as it might seem to some, but an act that appealed to a higher law of morality and justice. We had a dedication Mass of the new little estate, emphasising (I imagine) the virtues of solidarity and justice, followed by a simple celebration by candlelight – for as yet the men hadn't tapped the nearest electricity line.

Nor were isolated individuals alone party to such ways of proceeding. Faced with official unwillingness or inability, or incompetence, to provide schooling for the hordes of children that had converged with their families on Latin American cities – ostensibly because their occupation of private land was irregular – an organisation called 'Fe y Alegría' (Faith and Happiness), was established by a Venezuelan Jesuit for this specific purpose throughout the continent.

Many groups of religious, hearing the call of the bishops at Medellín, abandoned their prestige colleges in the cities for a simple dwelling amongst the teeming multitudes on the outskirts. They set about not only teaching children, but training adults and promoting community health, often with primitive resources, while the authorities learned to turn a blind eye to their ambiguous legal status. For four or five years in Medellín I, too, ranged round a dozen or so schools and communities, offering pastoral care and catechetical training. And thereby hangs a tale.

The text we were developing for the children was based on a rural programme where children were exploited for the mines. It was – as the term was – 'conscientising': taking the children's experience of their reality and confronting this with the scriptural message of freedom and justice in true community. The new bishop of Medellín – no friend of anything smacking of 'liberation' – eventually caught up with us and I had to seek employment elsewhere. For many, of course, this would be clear evidence that we were on the right track. For in the matter of 'option for the poor', the distance between institutional and pastoral practice within the church was still often considerable.

In the city of Cali now, in the south of Colombia, we began to hold weekly meetings in houses in the poorest sectors of the very poor parish. These took the form of a gospel reflection issuing in some specific action, followed by a simple eucharist and a little cup of black coffee together. Here, huddled together in dimly lit shacks, squatting on beds or boxes, people would hatch schemes like improving the precarious path running between the dwellings or improving the waste drainage that cascaded down the slopes. I recall joining a group of neighbours who were threatened with eviction from their illegal, but well-established, occupation of land by some city development plan. We attempted to lobby the official in charge. I remember feeling that she belonged to a different planet from the one I had been living on.

For this was the strange thing: as I settled into the rhythm of life in the marginalised world of Colombia, it felt somehow like being at the centre of the world. This was where the future lay, this was where the new hope for a better order of things would see the light of day following the difficult birth. Though the senses were continually assailed by sights, sounds and smells associated with the detritus of society, it was a privilege and a blessing to be there.

In addition, the sense of being part of a continent-wide community of purpose and commitment was a powerful support and motivator. We all belonged to an inexorable movement of change, each contributing our grain of sand in forgotten and hidden places, finding in our chance encounters that we spoke a common language, shared allies and enemies, knew each other's problems and hopes. There was a clear political and social project to establish a just society with which we could identify and to which owe allegiance.

III

I returned to Britain in time to 'see in' the year 1984 with its fateful overtones: the year of the trade union ban at the Communications Headquarters in Cheltenham; of police provocation and repression against striking miners; of the surrender of more English countryside for more US nuclear missile bases. The street riots of Brixton and Toxteth still smouldered; the Falklands victory had turned sour. I was back indeed not only a different person, but to a different Britain from the one I remembered leaving a decade or more earlier. What Bishop Sheppard of Liverpool called 'comfortable Britain' was losing touch with the other half. The social chasm was widening perceptibly, and hopelessness and resentment on one side was met by indifference and even contempt on the other.

It was in this 'other' Britain, a dwindling parish in a disintegrating part of inner-city Liverpool, where I now began to put down roots. I seemed to recognise instantly the world of ordinary human lives whom wealth, success and fortune pass by, whose humdrum existences were now marked by unemployment and apparent superfluity to the national enterprise. Here again, surely, were the friends I had already made, whose powerlessness is their greatest poverty, their humanity their greatest richness. Were these not the unwanted survivors of an era of material prosperity that had been built on the backs of their forebears and had now shrunk beyond their grasp? The grandchildren of the resilient and proud dockers and barrow-women who shaped Liverpool's character, they were now recipients of disdainful handouts and experimental housing in a city that had lost its reason for existing. Their communities had been broken up, their children's ambitions thwarted.

If there were a field ripe for applying the lessons of Latin America, surely it was here? I concluded. The agenda, after all, was not that different: encouraging people to feel and exercise their power, showing them that small gains in their quality of life could be achieved by concerted action, affirming their value and dignity in countless ways.

THE MEDELLIN DOCUMENT 41

My time in Liverpool happily coincided with the growth of community action and development in the neighbourhood. A broad coalition of community workers, local residents and church workers (myself and the local Anglican vicar included), met to oppose council plans to demolish a large group of terraced houses to make way for a new park. The people had not been asked. The locals of an adjacent ward had recently refused to be relocated and, taking control of political power, established what was to become the largest co-operative housing scheme in Europe. We resolved too to resist. After much lobbying and some nimble legal manoeuvrings – including organising a permanent squat – the decision was turned round, and a co-operative was formed which former residents were invited back to join.

The irony was, this was no Thatcherite regime we were dealing with, but the militant left whom we thought should in principle have been on the side of the people. It was a shock to discover that they knew, or wanted to know, as little about participation and consultation as did the government.

I had been used to being able to point the finger at this cruel despot, that corrupt system for situations of injustice. Here there seemed not even to be a clear 'us' and 'them'. And if 'us' can confront 'them', can 'them' also cooperate sometimes with 'us'? And if so, is it a question, basically, of getting the system's administrators and officials to act on behalf of those who constantly, constitutionally, fall through the net, and to see that this is in the best interests of all concerned in the long run? In other words, do we aim for replacement of society's unjust structures, or just plain reform?

The one element from the British scene that I missed, of course, was the weakness, even absence, of a clear gospel message and church commitment to the cause of human promotion and social justice. This was disconcerting to one who had lived where such a close link was taken for granted. The tension within the Latin American church had been between that sector wedded to the oligarchy, though reformed and modernised since

Vatican II, and that committed to the poor, radicalised and conscientised according to Medellín.

Here in Britain the tension seemed to be stalled somewhere between the old and the new, the traditionalist and the modernist. True, there were manifestations in word and deed within the churches of inconformity with the national state of affairs, as well as analysis from a Christian socialist perspective. But in the absence of any clearly articulated social project for the country, these tended to be uncoordinated and struggled to be taken seriously, most particularly, of course, when they appealed to the example of Latin America.

It was this sense of the dichotomy between faith and life, at least as perceived and expressed though I never believed as experienced, that drew some of us to reflect on the 'spirituality of the poor'. This was not spirituality 'for' the poor, however admirable attempts to provide this may be, but rather spirituality 'by' the poor. If faith must be 'inculturated' in the sense of emerging from, not merely adapted to, a culture, must this not also apply to the variety of social cultures in a polarised society like Britain?

For I came to believe firmly in what has been described as the 'culture of poverty' – the experience of being without or being excluded that provokes a set of responses to life's circumstances, and one's place in them, that is remarkably similar whether in the slums of Medellín or in an inner-city estate in Liverpool. The real point is not the degree of material deprivation (and one can argue for ever about who is poor and who isn't), but the awareness itself of being on the margin of things and of being able to do very little about it. This lack of access to social participation produces characteristic patterns of behaviour, values and world-view. So will not a faith – and its spirituality – that emerges from this experience be qualitatively different?

The virtues of this world of the margins, though often ignored or misunderstood, are not precisely the same as the virtues of the comfortable and secure. This suggests that its spirituality must be a paradigm of all spirituality, where a sense of dispossession and impotence is the absolute condition of our relationship with God. Not only that, but these virtues that survive in spite of the pressures of our fragmented and consumerist society, may have more to offer us than we imagine, who have become impoverished of vision and cynical of the possibility of radical change.

IV

And so to Northern Ireland at the beginning of 1998, that most intractable of imperialist colonies, and Portadown, that most sectarian of towns, where Protestants outnumber Catholics by 4 to 1, and denominations denote social and political allegiances as much as religious affiliation. It was in response to the call to work for justice by making an option for the poor that my Irish colleagues, over 20 years ago now, set up their house here in the Catholic sector of town. 'The Troubles' which started around 1968 – the year of Medellín – were fed by the radical protest and civil rights movements of the time, but discrimination and marginalisation against the Catholic/nationalist population had been endemic for decades. Moreover, the population had been traumatised by the wave of threats and violence that had swept through the streets of the Province during the 70s, resulting in the wholesale segregation of Catholic area from Protestant. It was a time for recovery, and the Jesuit community began to work with a double mission, that of community development and of reconciliation.

Looking back now, if some success can be claimed in the first, relative failure must be admitted in the second. Local residents were before long firmly in the driving seat in much of the neighbourhood organisation and activity, and before long began to employ workers to develop programmes and initiatives for the community, responsible to an elected management committee of which I am now a lowly member. We unassumingly play our part alongside others equally, perhaps more, competent than ourselves, and respond to issues as each feels best suited as part of a large team of volunteers.

On the other hand, in the late 1990s the historical and endemic bitterness and resentment between the two communities came to a head in the conflict over the Orange parade back from Drumcree church through the nationalist area. Prominent in giving voice to local opposition to this tradition were one or two Jesuits. In July of 1998 the authorities finally decided to prohibit the Orangemen's return route. The protests and violence resulting from this decision competed that summer with the World Cup for international TV coverage, and the Garvaghy Road momentarily became (according to one magazine) the 4th most famous street in the world.

Reconciliation or improving relations between communities thus became over these years if anything more difficult, more strained. A pensioners' group fails to turn up for a return Christmas party laid on by their Catholic counterparts; a Protestant youth club has its windows put in after it was rumoured they were going to invite Catholics in. Among the reasons, the impasse over the marching issue is the most obvious, but it is also true that the loyalist/unionist disenchantment and frustration has been allowed to fester since the signing of the Good Friday Agreement in 1998. Even among local clergy, Jesuits gained a reputation for stirring up trouble.

But 'community development' and 'reconciliation' – is there not an inconsistency implicit here? Opting for the poor entails seeing the world from their perspective, taking their part in their just cause. How can we do this and at the same time strive for some sort of accommodation with the oppressor? Can we be committed to one and yet detached from both? What if the oppressor feels himself to be oppressed too – where do we stand then? For it can be argued that both communities in Northern Ireland in fact share an experience of being beleaguered. With good reason or not, both feel they have had to fight for their very survival.

In this context, where does solidarity lie – with one? with the other? with both? with neither? perhaps at some point between the two? And if there is no true peace without justice – as I learnt from the message of Medellín – how can we reconcile ambivalent or competing claims of justice? And yet, if I withhold commitment from the just cause of either, in some allegedly higher interest of reconciliation, can I really affirm that I am committed to anybody?

These dilemmas have followed me into the field of mediation, where the belief prevails that conflicts can be mitigated, if not resolved, when people are willing to engage with one another with respect and honesty. Yet, 'Who holds the balance of power?' I find is frequently the question uppermost in my mind. But in Northern Ireland the imperative of reconciliation, prioritising action that heals differences and divisions, is presently, unquestionably, the urgent and paramount principle. Tossed to and fro between the rights and demands of each, one can occasionally glimpse in the gap the ideal of a higher, or deeper justice, where truth and compassion meet. In the struggle for liberation against oppression, how often have both oppressed and oppressor begun to resemble one another, liberating neither in the process?

V

During the second half of the 20th century the church in Latin America underwent an upheaval that entailed the realignment of commitments from wealth and power to the poor and marginalised. Tales of courage and the ensuing sacrifice inspired us in the church of the First World, and also intrigued us as to what they might have to teach us here. Yet this historical process that began with such promise seemed to end in so much pain. The 'rediscovery' of the gospel of the poor, heralded by the 1968 Medellín Conference of bishops, implemented in pastoral action throughout the region in subsequent decades, proclaimed by the popular church of revolutionary Nicaragua in 1979, and paid for by the blood of the Salvadoran martyrs amongst countless others, seems to survive now in the attenuated memories and hopes of small communities scattered throughout Brazil and elsewhere on the continent.

Nevertheless to us at least it has bequeathed precious concepts and principles with which to interpret and challenge the interface of faith and life: the gospel of liberation, the preferential option for the poor, the reality of structural sin in society, the historical task of constructing the kingdom, the conscientising role of evangelisation, the importance of basic Christian community. It has raised serious questions for our society and churches as well: are we too institutionally and ideologically bound to existing structures and systems of power? Do these determine our attitudes and behaviours towards those at the bottom of the social and economic pile? Have we 'inculturated' the pristine 'good news to the poor' into a middle-class western value-system?

But we are also left with more specific perplexities: Who – even where – are our poor? Who are their oppressors? are we, perchance? What are these unjust structures that must be changed? and what into? and how? Or will it be enough in a participative democracy like ours merely to reform or tamper with them to make them juster? How can we make the just struggle a reconciling one?

We may have looked across the ocean with, perhaps, a little longing – even envy – at the simple clear-cut scenario of villains and victims, and the clarity of vision and courage of conviction that characterised its heroes and martyrs. We may have wondered whether our own world and its churches were just too tired and set in their ways to contemplate any sort of upheaval, or simply too scared.

I have not proposed suggestions or solutions to these doubts and questions. Still less put forward the Latin American experience as model for our own culture and faith context. What I have aimed to do was take you on a journey with me over the past 30 years through Latin America, back to Britain and finally to Northern Ireland. I have tried to focus on aspects of a story that, indeed, taught me many things – about pastoral action in favour of justice, for instance – but that modified during its course many of the clarities and certainties of those early, heady, years.

THE MEDELLIN DOCUMENT 47

To put it another way, I wanted to address the question of how to translate the witness of the Latin American church, as articulated in one key document that set out its social teaching, into the terms of our own culture and experience by looking through the eyes of one particular, if not particularly significant, pilgrim.

All I can say is, that had I not gone through the refining fire there myself (or was it a cauldron?), that sharpened my awareness and concentrated my commitment, I am certain I would hardly have known back in Britain how or where to begin – how work for justice, where find the poor. But that may say more about myself than about Latin America. As I see it, I had the good fortune to be in the right place at the right time, and the lessons I learnt there have served me well ever since as I strove to make sense of my surroundings.

CHAPTER FOUR

Subsidiarity and the Family

Finola Kennedy

It might be appropriate if I could begin by saying that the social teaching of the church has had some direct influence on my personal life. But it would be untrue. I hope that the gospel teaching about loving one's neighbour has had some influence. I can think of no more radical social framework than the idea of the church as the Body of Christ, but the corpus of 'social teaching' as promulgated in a series of encyclicals from *Rerum Novarum* onwards has impinged on me only indirectly. In my work as an economist I have studied the development of the welfare state and of family change in relation to economic change. Study in these areas led me to a studyof relevant Catholic social teaching. What I discovered was a well from which to draw; not a stagnant well, rather one founded on a spring. Despite periodic claims to immutability, I did not find a static body of teaching; rather one which contained an element of development and change.

Prior to the pontificate of Leo XIII, the popes did not focus much on what could be described as social questions. With Leo, the Roman attitude towards democracy and to modern industrialisation, changed significantly. In 1891, *Rerum Novarum* provided a critique of both socialism and capitalism. While it defended the right to private property, it also defended the rights of workers to a living wage and to organise in trade unions. By the time *Quadragesimo Anno* was published, totalitarian clouds were gathering and private ownership was viewed as a necessary means to achieving the common good. *Quadragesimo Anno* proposed the principle of subsidiarity, of the state granting help (*subsidium*) to, but not replacing smaller bodies, foremost of which was the family. I will return to this.

By the time John XXIII published *Mater et Magistra*, the need for a better relationship between rich and poor countries is addressed. The right to property is made subject to the right of all mankind to the necessities of life. *Pacem in Terris* continues to take a more global view and is prepared to condemn capitalism as defective in many respects. The first hand experience of Pope John Paul II of living under a communist régime, shifts the spotlight unto the defects of such régimes.

In this article I plan to focus on the concept of 'subsidiarity' and its significance in setting the context for an understanding of the family in Ireland. The concept of subsidiarity was developed in the German Koeningswinter Circle, a group of Catholic intellectuals interested in political economy who had a major influence on the author of *Quadragesimo Anno*, the Jesuit priest, Oswald Von Nell-Breuning, and on the evolution of Christian democracy in pre- and post-war Germany.[1] It is a concept which has been embraced, in recent decades, at EU level, as Christian democratic ideas have percolated the Union, and acted as a counterbalance to excessive central control and direction.

The core of *Quadragesimo Anno* was an emphasis on the individual human person as both the source and end of society. The purpose of social relationships and of human communities is to give help, *subsidium*, to individuals as they realise their human development. The state should not, except in exceptional circumstances, remove or replace the individual; rather the state should try to provide the conditions for the exercise of individual responsibility. Decision-making should be at the 'lowest' possible level in society. The key passage in the encyclical is the following:

> It is true, as history clearly shows, that because of changed circumstances much that formerly was performed by small associations can now be accomplished only by larger ones.

---

1. George Weigel (1992), 'Catholicism and Democracy: The Other Twentieth-Century Revolution', in G. L. Anderson and M. A. Kaplan (eds), *Morality and Religion in Liberal Democratic Societies*, Paragon House, New York, p 232.

Nevertheless, it is a fixed and unchangeable principle, most basic in social philosophy, unmoveable and unalterable, that, just as it is wrong to take away from individuals what they can accomplish by their own ability and efforts and then entrust it to a community, so it is an injury and at the same time both a serious evil and a disturbance of right order to assign to a larger and higher society what can be performed successfully by smaller and lower communities. The reason is that all social activity of its very power and nature, should supply help (subsidium) to the members of the social body, but may never destroy or absorb them.

This sort of thinking informed the Irish Constitution of 1937. In his study of the Constitution, John Kelly describes Articles 41 and 42 which deal with the Family and with Education as being among the most innovative in the entire Constitution.[2] The Constitution of 1922 contained nothing about the family and marriage. The thinking in *Quadragesimo Anno* influenced education, health and social welfare policy, where church teaching stressed that the state had the right to intervene only in a subsidiary capacity. The small farmers who formed a large segment of the community, and who had recently won the right to land ownership, were not attracted to socialism, and were wary of an extended role for the state. Kevin O'Higgins remarked, 'We were probably the most conservative minded revolutionaries that ever put through a successful revolution.'[3]

The principle of subsidiarity was one which appealed to the new small proprietors in post-Independence Ireland, and which suited de Valera's purposes; by supporting the principle of subsidiarity, de Valera was both following the church teaching, and endorsing the principle of private ownership which, after generations of exclusion, was embedded in the Irish psyche. A comparison of the text of Article 41 of the Constitution with extracts from papal encyclicals shows a virtual identity. Article 41.1.1 says:

---

2. John Kelly (1980), *The Irish Constitution*, Jurist Publishing Company, Dublin, p. 483.
3. Joe Lee (1989), *Ireland 1912-1985,* 105, Cambridge University Press.

The State recognises the Family as the natural primary and fundamental unit group of society – as a moral institution possessing inalienable and imprescriptible rights, antecedent and superior to all positive law.

This echoes Leo XIII in *Rerum Novarum*:

The family is a society limited, indeed in numbers, but no less a true society, anterior to every kind of State or nation, invested with rights and duties of its own, totally independent of the civil community.

Article 41.1.2° says:

The State, therefore, guarantees to protect the Family in its constitution and authority, as the necessary basis of social order and as indispensable to the welfare of the Nation and the State.

This would certainly meet with the approval of Pius XI who wrote in *Casti Connubii:*

Those who have the care of the State and of the common good cannot neglect the needs of married people without bringing great harm upon the State and upon the common welfare.

The phrase 'social order' in Article 41.1.2° merits comment, echoing as it does, *Quadragesimo Anno,* known as the Encyclical on the Social Order. In the *Preamble* to the Constitution, the attainment of 'true social order' is one of the objectives for which the Constitution is adopted. The phrase 'social order' also appears in Article 45.1 regarding the Directive Principles of Social Policy, as well as in Article 41.1.2°

Articles 41.2.1° and 41.2.2° say:

In particular the State recognises that by her life within the home, woman gives to the State, a support without which the common good cannot be achieved.

The State shall, therefore, endeavour to ensure that mothers shall not be obliged by economic necessity to engage in labour to the neglect of their duties in the home.

These sentiments fit perfectly with those of Pius XI:

> Intolerable and to be opposed with all our strength is the abuse whereby mothers of families, because of the insufficiency of the father's salary, are forced to engage in gainful occupations outside the domestic walls, to the neglect of their proper cares and duties, particularly the education of their children *(Quadragesimo Anno)*.

According to Pius XI a first duty of the state in providing for the common good is to protect and strengthen family life,

> Not only in those things which regard temporal goods is it the concern of public authority that proper provision be made for matrimony and the family, but also in matters pertaining to the good of souls: namely, just laws should be made for the protection of chastity, for reciprocal conjugal aid, and for similar purposes *(Casti Connubii: 62)*.

This Papal teaching would certainly fit in with Articles 41.3.1° and 41.3.2°:

> The State pledges itself to guard with special care the institution of Marriage, on which the Family is founded, and to protect it against attack
>
> No law shall be enacted providing for the grant of a dissolution of marriage.

The implication that the proper sphere of women's activity was the home, and that women should be limited to that sphere, was at the root of much of the criticism of the references to women in the Constitution and sparked a campaign against the draft Constitution which contained the phrase, 'the inadequate strength of women'. The campaign, mainly from middle-class women, was led by the National University Women Graduates' Association, the Irish Women Workers' Union, the Standing Committee on Legislation Affecting Women, and the Joint

SUBSIDIARITY AND THE FAMILY

Committee of Women's Societies and Social Workers representing more than a dozen women's Groups.[4] Speaking in the Dáil during the debates on the Constitution, de Valera defended himself against the criticisms of women's organisations, arguing at length that the object of the references to women in the draft Constitution were protective.[5] De Valera further claimed – and the claim was made at a time when legislative measures did in fact prevent the employment of married women as national teachers and in the civil service – 'There is no suggestion that women should be stopped from entering into avocations for which they have aptitude or will or desire'.[6]

The Mother and Child crisis of the early 1950s left church teaching on the family exposed to criticism and, arguably, the combined victory of the medical profession and the Catholic hierarchy in seeing off what they believed to be unwarranted intervention in the family, exposed a vein of anti-clericalism in Ireland which would permeate the entire body politic in the coming decades. The Mother and Child victory was to prove a pyrrhic one with too great a cost for the clergy, as seeds were sown for the alienation of their strongest supporters – women.

Two examples serve to illustrate the form of Catholic teaching which helped to scupper the Mother and Child scheme. One is contained in the writing of a Jesuit priest in the 1940s, the other in a statement of the hierarchy in 1950. In 1943, following the publication of the Beveridge Report the previous year, an influential symposium was held by the Statistical and Social Inquiry Society of Ireland. In his paper to the Symposium, entitled,'The Ethical Aspect', Fr Coyne SJ expressed concern about state intrusion in family life, saying:

> The second great danger of certain types of social services from a moralist's point of view is that men may easily lose moral stamina ... Hunger or its fear, the love of wife and fam-

---

4. *Irish Press*, 11 May 1937.
5. Dáil Debates, Vol 67, Col 67, 11 May 1937.
6. Dáil Debates, Vol 67, Col 71, 11 May 1937.

ily, the hope of a secure old age are nature's way of calling forth the best that is in man.'[7]

A classical statement of subsidiarity is to be found in a letter dated 10 October 1950 from the Catholic hierarchy to the then Taoiseach, John A. Costello. It was written in the context of the Mother and Child controversy and subsequently published in *The Irish Times:*

> The right to provide for the health of the children belongs to parents, not to the State. The State has the right to intervene only in a subsididary capacity to supplement, not to supplant. It may help indigent or neglectful parents; it may not deprive ninety per cent of parents of their rights because of ten per cent necessitous or negligent parents (*The Irish Times*, 13 October 1951).

Much has changed since 1931, when *Quadragesimo Anno* was published, as might be illustrated by the difference in thinking of Fr Coyne in the 1940s and Fr Sean Healy of CORI, in 2004. One could not imagine Fr Coyne on the road to Inchidoney. Yet Brendan Walsh has made the perceptive observation that in the late 1950s:

> The Irish Catholic hierarchy were very hostile to any measures that could be interpreted as socialist. The preference for 'voluntarism' over 'bureaucracy' led them to oppose the extension of state activity or control in areas such as health and education. The welfare state was condemned because the philosophy behind it conflicted with that contained in Papal Encyclicals.[8]

But, according to Walsh, 'By the 1970s several bishops were arguing that the state had a duty to use the tax and social welfare

---

7. Fr John Coyne SJ,'The Ethical Aspect', Contribution to Symposium on the Beveridge Report, Journal ofthe Statistical and Social Inguiry Society of Ireland, 1943.
8. Brendan Walsh (1986), 'The Growth of Government', Kieran A. Kennedy, *Ireland in Transition*, The Mercier Press, p 62.

system to tackle the poverty and inequality that were widespread in Ireland.'[9]

Much has changed since the Irish Constitution was passed into law in 1937. The Constitution itself has been subject to a raft of amendments, the most important of which, in the current context, is the introduction of divorce following a referendum in 1995. As a result, the definition of the family in the Constitution as founded on 'the institution of marriage' has changed. From the perspective of the civil law, as distinct from the canon law of the church, marriage is no longer necessarily for life and, *inter alia*, pensions, property and childcare must be adapted to a changed context. Because a marriage can now be ended legally under certain conditions at the request of one of the parties, and this is provided for in the Constitution, lone parents can be created as a result of a constitutional provision.

Further change has been wrought by the emergence into the public domain of the dark side of the family, including incest and every form of abuse. In many cases the individual needs to be protected from the family. Therefore, it seems to me that the idea, proposed by Leo XIII in *Rerum Novarum*, that the family is 'totally independent of civil society' cannot be held as an absolute value. There has been a seismic shift in the public perception of the role of women since the Constitution was promulgated in 1937. At that time, the primary role of women was seen as creators and sustainers of the home. This is very far indeed from Budget 2000 which sought to incentivise the movement of women into the workplace via taxation changes in order to meet market shortages. If one looks at the enshrinement of the 'woman in the home' in the Constitution, I would argue that the opposite economic motivation existed on that occasion, i.e. to keep women out of the workforce in order to reserve the limited number of jobs available to men.

Partly due to the growth in the participation of married women and mothers in the workforce, there has been a steady

---

9. Walsh, ibid, p 66.

drift towards the institutionalisation of childcare and of elder care. Creches and nursing homes for the elderly are everywhere in demand. More and more the provision of these facilities is seen as the responsibility of the state. As the institutionalisation of dependants proceeds apace, one may wonder if some insights of the social teaching of the 1950s have been lost. One does not hear nowadays about home duties, no more than filial duty.

Leo XIII's description of the family in *Rerum Novarum* as a society 'anterior to every kind of State or nation', finds an echo in John Paul II's description of the family as 'the primordial and, in a certain sense sovereign society', in his Letter to Families in 1994. This is more nuanced than the claim of Leo's that the family is totally independent of civil society. Pope John Paul II has shown a deep and constant concern for families and family life. The first synod of John Paul's reign in 1980 was on the family. Change has entered into the picture with endorsement by the church of woman's role in the economy. In his recent *Letter on the Collaboration between Men and Women*, Cardinal Ratzinger speaks of 'the irreplaceable role of women in all aspects of family and social life involving human relationships and caring for others'.[10] This implies the significant and active presence of women in the family. But, Ratzinger continues:

> It means also that women should be present in the world of work and in the organisation of society, and that women should have access to positions of responsibility which allow them to inspire the policies of nations and to promote innovative solutions to economic and social problems (Ratzinger, 2004).

Cardinal Ratzinger then goes on to say:

> The harmonisation of the organisation of work and laws governing work with the demands stemming from the mission

---

10. Cardinal Ratzinger (2004), *Letter to the Bishops of the Catholic Church on the Collaboration of Men and Women in the Church and in the World.*

of women within the family is a challenge. The question is not only legal, economic and organisational; it is above all a question of mentality, culture, and respect. (ibid.)

The harmonisation of the organisation of work with what Cardinal Ratzinger calls 'the mission of women within the family' is indeed a challenge. One wonders what would Pius XI think? Would he think that the situation has arrived where the family cannot function without substantial intervention by the state? Or could it be, that he would continue to argue, as *Quadragesimo Anno* did, that if functions which can be undertaken by smaller societies, in this case, care of children by families, are taken over by the state, then families will be absorbed or destroyed? It is only possible to speculate.

At a time when pressure is mounting on the state for assistance with child care, in the form of more creches, it is clear that the social teaching, although stressing the need to respect the work of the woman in the home, has developed to an awareness of the balance between the home and the workplace. However, there is missing in the teaching a development of the role of men in the home as fathers. Perhaps that will be the next development.

CHAPTER FIVE

Retreat of the Father

Paul Andrews SJ

This is complicated. I am writing about fatherhood, but I am not a father. And although I am not a father, I am habitually addressed as Father, unlike most fathers. It is a sign of how loaded with symbolism the term Father is: much more than a biological relationship, it carries momentous overtones.

To see what the church has to say about fatherhood, I suppose we should look first at the scriptures, where two fathers dominate: God and St Joseph. The Bible is the story of a family, framed in terms of the father rather than the mother. Of all the words that Jesus spoke, the ones most commonly repeated by his followers are the prayer that begins 'Our Father'. Jesus took a big gamble when he spoke of our father in heaven. God is beyond gender, beyond our imagination. He is a spirit, with no body, so in calling him male or female we are projecting our own mortal notions onto the immortal and invisible. Moreover, if we have bad associations or memories of either father or mother, we risk contaminating our idea of God with them.

That is where Jesus took the gamble. Those who have known a father as a tyrant or drunkard, will have strange connotations to the words 'our father in heaven'. If Jesus had spoken of 'our mother in heaven', he would have run a similar risk. No human words are as heavily charged with emotional overtones as father and mother. It is only when we move away from home, and reflect on our history, that after many years we begin to see what mother and father did to us, for better or worse. When we do, some of our religious attitudes and feelings start to make sense.

All through our life we are trying to sort out our sense of our heavenly father/mother. Jesus always speaks of his father. We see what he meant in the parable of the prodigal son, in which the central figure is the merciful father. In that extraordinary and moving story, Jesus comes nearest to giving us a picture of God.

For some of us, the memory of father may be of an absentee, as happens more and more often today: the father who begets a child and then disappears, not even giving his name to the child. In Ireland a third of our first-born children are in that state, not carrying their father's name. Of all the revelations from our Central Statistics Office, many of them bringing us good cheer about productivity and economic growth, that figure is the one that should give us pause. About one in three of the eldest children in new families, knows father only as an absentee, someone who begot them and vanished. He remains a role-model (especially for his sons) whether he wants to or not. In the child's phantasy there is no such thing as a single parent. The other one, the missing one, remains as a shadowy icon.

St Augustine, in a memorable Latin phrase, insists that God is not like that. *Non enim fecit atque abiit.* He did not just make us and go away. He works with us and for us, and we see his hand not just in the sunshine and obvious blessings, but even in the dark times, in our sorrowful mysteries. He is always present to us. The prodigal's father stayed on at home even after what his older son and neighbours (and maybe his wife too) would have seen as the enormous folly of letting the younger boy loose with money. When the prodigal returned, his father was waiting and watching, there when he was needed.

For some of us father may have been someone we could not talk to. I knew a 16-year-old who complained: 'I have not spoken to my father for eighteen months. Whenever I have something I want to talk to him about, he will be starting into a TV programme that he says he has to watch, and tells me to come back later.' I asked the boy: 'What happened 18 months ago?' He smiled: 'There was a power cut. We had no lights or TV, so we sat round a candle and played cards. It was the best family evening for years.'

We don't have to wait for a power cut to talk to God. He can be part of our breathing in and breathing out. He is listening when we turn to him, no matter how we are dressed, or how we are behaving, or what we have done in the past week. When we turn to him in prayer, he is there waiting, happy to see us. When you pray, go to your private room, and when you have shut your door, pray to your father who is in that secret place, and your father who sees all that is done in secret will reward you ... Your father knows what you need before you ask him (Mt 6:6).

For some of us, father was someone you could not mess with, maybe a perfectionist, who got uptight about any failing in his children: somebody who was slow to bless but easily disappointed or annoyed. Turn again to the parable: the prodigal son messed up his father in a way anyone could have warned him about. Normally sons worked for their father till he died. Then the estate was divided. Some would say the prodigal's father was doting, giving away the inheritance ahead of time. Anyone could have told him it would be squandered – and so it was. He allowed the son to make his mistakes, but kept a place for him in his heart. This is a picture not so much of a foolish old man, as of the one who knows what is in our hearts and is unsurprisable.

God sees us as his children. It is unthinkable for a mother not to love her baby, or for God not to love us. He delights in us as his children, no matter what our age, no matter what mistakes we have made. The parable of the prodigal ends with a party. The older brother was upset – this was making too much fuss of the young rascal. He missed the point. The father threw it to express his own joy at having his son back again.

Here is the model

No textbook could match this parable in portraying the qualities of a father vividly and succinctly. He is not overprotective. He allows his son the freedom to follow his own dream rather than his father's, to take risks and to make mistakes. He is still there for the son who has made a fool of himself and brought shame on the family. He absorbs the jealousy and anger of the older son but does not yield to him. He shows what it is to be a man: there when he is needed; faithful to wife and children; able for lifelong commitment; nurturant, forgiving, patient, and aware that children can learn from their mistakes.

Saint Joseph: what do we know?
The other key father in the New Testament is Joseph. What do we know about St Joseph? That he loved Mary so much that he suppressed his doubts about her chastity and allowed himself to be regarded as the father of her child, knowing that he wasn't (when Jesus took the floor in the Nazareth synagogue (Luke 4:22), the begrudgers remarked: Is not this the son of Joseph?); that he brought up that child as his own, despite great difficulties and dangers, particularly at the start; that he taught him his trade; that he loved him; and that Jesus' virile health (physical stamina, courage, strength of purpose and attractiveness to women, men and children) as an adult is proof of good parenting by his foster-father. Joseph is the obvious patron of adoptive fathers.

I would not paint Joseph
The iconography of the western church is centred round mother and child, not father and child. Perhaps Joseph's unique role in the history of salvation has made it harder for artists to show Jesus and his foster-father. Jean-Paul Sartre, in his Christmas play *Barjona*, imagines himself painting the nativity scene:

> And Joseph? I would not paint Joseph. I would show no more than a shadow at the back of the stable, and two shining eyes. For I do not know what to say about Joseph, and Joseph does not know what to say about himself. He adores, and is happy to adore, and he feels himself slightly out of it. I believe he suffers without admitting it. He suffers because he sees how much this woman whom he loves resembles God; how she is already at the side of God. For God has burst like a bomb into the intimacy of this family. Joseph and Mary are separated for ever by this explosion of light. And I imagine that all through his life Joseph will be learning to accept this.

John Paul II

Skip two thousand years to Pope John Paul II, who in 1981 wrote a letter known as *Familiaris Consortio*, about the Christian family in the modern world. Section 25 deals with fathers, and focuses on three qualities:

1. fidelity to a wife;
2. care of children;
3. the sort of presence in the family that is neither oppressively dominant (the Pope uses the word *machismo*, as though he was thinking of Roddy Doyle's *Charlo*) nor leaving everything to the wife.

None of the three can be taken for granted in Ireland today. Though they may sound like pious exhortations, they are in fact meaty.

Wife, partner, lover

The Pope mentions fidelity to a wife. Do we need marriage? Some commentators find the use of the terms wife, husband, spouse embarrassing and politically incorrect. Advertisements for lotteries and competitions offer prizes to you and your partner. Now partner is a good word with a strong meaning: a person who has agreed to work with you in some area of life, such as golf or cards, business or politics. Our present Taoiseach has a partner, Mary Harney. Many firms in law or industry carry the names of two or three partners.

Then what do you call the woman who shares your bed without the contract of marriage? The Chinese spoke of concubines, the Victorian middle classes of mistresses. We have a good word which denotes both the bond of affection and its transient nature: lover. There is more at stake here than just language usage. When words like spouse, marriage, wife or husband become politically incorrect (i.e. when the faint-hearted fear to use them in public), the family is devalued. There is a cheapening of the life-commitment that marriage implies, and that gives stability to the personality and growth of children.

Cohabitation or marriage

A partner may object: 'We all know that it is better for children to grow up in a secure relationship, but that doesn't mean the couple has to be married.' Wrong. That's exactly what it does mean. Cohabitations break down much more frequently than marriages and also make subsequent marriages unstable. Only 36% of children born to partners are still looked after by both parents – even if they eventually marry – by the time the children are 16, compared with 70% of children born to married couples. Generally speaking, children suffer permanent disadvantage if their parents aren't together when they grow up. Of course, some such children emerge relatively unscathed; but to tell the public that other types of family are just as successful for children as married parents is simply a lie. The immense research on this issue points one way. Halsey, an ethical socialist, summed up the evidence: 'The children of parents who do not follow the traditional norm ... tend to die earlier, to have more illness, to do less well in school, to exist at a lower level, to be more prone to deviance and crime, and finally to repeat the cycle of unstable parenting from which they themselves suffered.'

So when John Paul II emphasises fidelity to a wife, he is not just taking a moral position, but leaning on a mass of experience and research evidence.

Fathers and Children

The dire consequences of the retreat of the father have been analysed above all by Jacques Lacan:

> In the majority of neuroses of our time we can designate the principal determinant in the personality of the father who is always lacking in some way or another, absent or humiliated, divided or sham.

John Paul II is in the same camp (*Familiaris Consortio* 25):

> Where social and cultural conditions so easily encourage a father to be less concerned with his family, or at any rate less involved in the work of education, efforts must be made to

restore socially the conviction that the place and task of the father in and for the family is of unique and irreplaceable importance. As experience teaches, the absence of a father causes psychological and moral imbalance and notable difficulties in family relations, as does, in contrary circumstances, the oppressive presence of a father, especially where there still prevails the phenomenon of machismo, or a wrong superiority of male prerogatives which humiliates women and inhibits the development of healthy family relationships.

It is fifty years since Bowlby noted that the securest babies are those who have seen a lot of their fathers; forty years since Schaffer and Emerson found that for nearly one third of infants, the main attachment was with their father. Since then, more and more research has documented the special contribution of fathers to their children. Given the opportunity, they can be as nurturant of young children, as capable and emotionally responsive, as mothers are.

Though many fathers feel themselves as failures, out of touch with their children and over-busy, their impact on the family is still profound. The effects of contact with father are in securer babies, and children who are intellectually curious and independent, ready to explore and take risks. Involvement of fathers influences their children's sex-role development and academic performance. Poor father-child relationships are strongly associated with delinquency in sons.

Greally in USA, and researchers in Belgium and Australia, were surprised to find that in terms of the child's religious commitment, father seems to have a stronger influence than mother: perhaps for this reason: if a young person associates religion primarily with prayers-at-mother's-knee and the lessons of early childhood, it is liable to be left behind in the youngster's determination to put away the things of a child. But if religious commitment, a sense of prayer and responsibility to one's maker, is seen in the father, who is making his way in a harsh and competitive society (and it is still the case that children are more likely to see their father than their mother as the bread-winner outside the home), then the young person is more likely to see faith as part of the challenge of adult life than as a relic of childhood.

Once again research supports the Pope.

The father's presence
The presence of a father to his family is obviously more than physical. Essentially it means that his wife and children have a place in his mind, and he in theirs. It sometimes requires years, or even decades, before we taste exactly what that presence means to us. A man may have a deep affection for his family, but be unable to show it, and then is blamed for not showing it. He can be bad-mouthed or caricatured in family talk, yet individual family members retain a sense of him that goes beyond caricature. Roddy Doyle has given a brilliant picture of such a son in *Paddy Clarke ha ha ha*.

The Pope comments that social and cultural conditions easily encourage a father to be less concerned with his family. Jacques Lacan, that profound but obscure observer of family relationships, saw the retreat of the father as the greatest danger to western civilisation. The retreat may show itself in focusing on work outside the home, and confining his role to providing for the family, leaving all the effective decisions to his wife. He may never have recovered from the shattering post-natal discovery of what a change children make in the lives of their parents, and shied away from taking part or making his voice heard in the home. It may be a more total retreat, refusing any commitment to his children or their mother. Or it may be the sort of retreat involved in separation or divorce, which can leave the displaced father feeling discouraged, deskilled and emasculated. Our Constitution, sometimes thought of as patriarchal, is curiously silent about fathers; those who have lost their children can find themselves at a huge disadvantage in law. Both men and women are diminished by a Constitution that over-identifies women with motherhood and under-identifies men with fatherhood.

Sorry, single mothers

Dear single mothers, you may have read these pages with increasing irritation. You may feel that the emphasis on the father's role implies impoverishment in the single-parent families you rear, often with heroic generosity. But even at the risk of offending, the issue is too important and painful to allow either personal emotion or political correctness to interfere. Our task is to discern the realities for children, whether or not it is politically correct to do so, or makes people feel guilty. Single mothers, whose children have no resident father, can feel threatened when confronted with the findings of observation and research. No matter what the topic, if one generalises about the effect of certain conditions on children, some people will feel guilty and resentful.

The point of the debate is precisely to foresee the dangers and obviate them. If fatherless boys suffer from the absence of a male model, that need can be partly met in various ways: grandparents, uncles, older brothers, teachers or others can become effective father-figures, men who have a place for the child in their mind and heart, and who model what it is to be a man. Children are adaptable and use help where they can find it.

The effect of father-absence on daughters is more subtle. They always have, in their mother, a model of what it is to be a woman. It is probably this strength that makes girls so problem-free relative to boys – the latter outnumber girls at least three to one in referrals to child guidance clinics. But a father helps in other ways: his unpossessive love and admiration for his daughter can give her a confidence in her own attractiveness. Research also shows fathers as giving their daughters – and their sons – greater intellectual curiosity and independence.

The nuclear family offers a space for the extraordinary tensions that arise out of intimate living: between man and wife, father and son, mother and daughter, brothers and sisters. The Bible, from Cain and Abel on, is the story of such tensions. Within a family these explosive forces can be worked through in a framework of exceptional strength. Even the revolts of adolescence are negotiated successfully in 90% of families, because of the bond of unsentimental affection that binds parents to one another and to their children. The result is a dynamic equilibrium, which produces a particular sort of people. To quote Lacan again: 'If you want an institution that will produce a creative and revolutionary people, there is none to compare with the western nuclear family.'

Some may feel that it is an undesirable goal: that we would be better off with unimaginative and conformist citizens. But if we base our most fundamental social unit on the desire to avoid conflict or disagreement, the result will be different and probably less effective. The achievements of civilisation are built on harnessing tensions, not avoiding them. The family is not just one of our social institutions, but the one on which all others depend; it affects how we grow our children. The teaching of the church, based on scripture, is not so much about the impoverishment of single-parent families, as about the enrichment that two parents can offer.

CHAPTER SIX

Catholic Social Teaching and DORAS Luimní

Ann Scully RSM

For many years now the Christian churches have tried to give a voice to those who are voiceless, among whom are people who are poor, who are sick and who are refugees. In these times there is an overriding need to be concerned for, and take care of, people seeking asylum or refugee status in our world. As one poster says 'Christians should know a thing or two about refugees ... their founder was one.' (Mt 2:13-23) The flight into Egypt is a story which has introduced Christians from earliest times to the reality of people seeking refuge and safety, and of our obligation to provide that security and protection in a more safe and less traumatic situation than would have been their experience. Like Jesus, Mary and Joseph they should be afforded that protection until it is safe to go back to their own place.

Refugees need protection. This means preventing refugees from being returned to a country where they may be in danger of persecution, and promoting their rights in such fields as accommodation, education, employment and freedom of movement.

In Europe over the past number of years European Union countries have been developing and harmonising their asylum/ refugee and immigration policies. This is happening in the context of EU enlargement, an EU Constitution, and political, economic and military developments. The EU is also developing its trade and other relationships with, for example, Africa. Meanwhile many of the countries of Africa are at war internally for a number of years. These wars, the implications of trade relationships and the repayment of debt to the World Bank are creating situations in Africa and elsewhere leading to major displacement of peoples. Wars especially are creating huge numbers of refugees, within countries, in neighbouring countries and further afield in stable countries such as EU states.

The church has always had something to say about crisis situations. As the church's social teaching has developed over the years, the emphasis has sometimes been on one aspect and then another and, perhaps because the issue being treated didn't touch our immediate experience, we may not have noticed the content. With our present experience, we may now have to re-read such documents with more aware and mature eyes and heart.

The social teaching of the church is about creating a just society as well as a more caring and charitable society. In dealing with refugees and people seeking asylum we need to ensure that we are not just nice, charitable, benevolent people, but brothers and sisters who constantly work so that the life and dignity of the person is protected. This puts an onus on us to be aware of the human rights and the legal entitlements of people. Charity is not enough and often it lets governments off the hook in ensuring that people's legal entitlements are upheld. It is our duty in this area to ensure that states and their agencies work to resolve existing refugee problems and to prevent new ones from developing.

DORAS Luimní, of which I am a member, came about due to the Irish Government's announcement, in late 1999, of a policy of 'dispersal and direct provision.' It was obvious that Limerick, being a major city, would become a centre for people in the asylum process.

I had learned from doing preparatory work with local communities in other parts of Ireland that unfounded fears, rumours and hearsay take people over. In such situations people say and do things that create an environment that can make life for people in the asylum process almost unbearable. In Limerick, therefore, it was important to be pro-active rather than reactive in this situation. *DORAS Luimní* (Development Organisation for Refugees and Asylum Seekers) came into being to offer friendship and support to people who came seeking for asylum, to be a bridge with the local community, to work with local and national statutory service providers and to encourage the government to implement humane and compassionate policies. All this ties in with the gospel call to welcome the stranger.

In Catholic social teaching, the 1963 document *Pacem in Terrris* of Pope John XXIII emphasises the value of human existence and everything necessary to make life comfortable and respectful of human dignity. In line with this aspect of the social teaching, groups like *DORAS* monitor the Direct Provision Centres to ensure that, within the strict Department of Justice guidelines, life is respected, that people are no longer afraid for their safety and that adequate food, shelter and clothing is available. This also entails ensuring that people from differing ethnic or religious backgrounds who may have been at war in their country of origin, do not end up in the same hostels or indeed sharing rooms with each other as happens on rare occasions. These kinds of details are often only available or come to prominence at local level and need to be adequately dealt with to ensure the safety of people and to ensure that people will not again be traumatised where they have sought safety.

The right to emigrate and to immigrate and the right of political refugees to migrate, are specifically addressed in *Pacem in Terris*, which teaches that refugees should be not just tolerated but enabled to enter into the life of the community, especially the political life. In 2003 Ireland held local elections. All people residing in Ireland on a certain date had a right to vote in these elections. This included migrant workers, asylum seekers, refugees, and people who were temporary residents for whatever reason. It fell to groups like *DORAS* to open the doors and ensure that the blocks – administratively and legally – were removed and these people were enabled to exercise their franchise. In *Pacem in Terris* we are exhorted to be involved in such activity. These same articles, (26, 27) would, as a result of the citizenship referendum and the resultant ministerial declaration of 1 January 2005, oblige us to challenge the procedures affecting children born to people in the asylum process who later attain refugee recognition and, as a consequence, relinquish their citizenship of their country of origin. These children when born assume the nationality of their parents so, when that nationality is relinquished, the situation in relation to the child needs to be clarified. The teaching of John Paul II on the family, *Familiaris Consortio* (1981), also puts our obligations and responsibilities in the area of the protection of the family unit and of children. This area alone is deserving of a separate paper. The ideal of human solidarity involves us automatically in the lives and rights of such people. What unites us in this whole area is our common humanity.

Art as a means to social solidarity
Pacem in Terris, among other later documents, draws attention to valuing cultural difference and to having the freedom to express such differences. In *DORAS Luimní* we have discovered the enormous richness of such cultural differences; we have learned how to express difference and how to develop the talents of people irrespective of language or cultural barriers. We are very lucky in that one of our volunteers happens to be a member of the staff of the World Music Centre at University of Limerick, and another happens to be an artist. Through these contacts and with this expertise available, DORAS has been able to facilitate the development and expression of musicians and artists from around the world. The talents of these people might otherwise have remained dormant and undiscovered, and we would all have been so much less enriched. Through art and music we have also been able to portray a very positive and inspirational aspect of immigration and asylum seeking which off-sets some of the negative stereotyping of people and the negative, racist attitudes and actions that are raising their ugly heads in Ireland at the moment.

These artists have introduced us to worlds that many of us would never have dreamed of before. Many of them paint out of their experience in their country of origin and so we learn through art of the social, economic and political realities in those countries. One person painted a fascinating mosaic of a scene in his country of origin. A particular feature of this work was women's faces. In his country of origin he would have been beheaded for this painting. This little detail brought home to all something of the oppressive regimes we hear about but often cannot comprehend – that this is reality. These works of art have gone on display in areas from Co Clare through Limerick and to Kilkenny. In each of these places cultural expressions are brought into the lives of people who might otherwise never go to an art gallery and be introduced to such diverse views of the world.

Art can also help to cross socio-economic and cultural boundaries. The clientele of the Limerick Youth Services comes from deprived areas of Limerick city. Some of the people in the asylum process were invited to be students in some of their courses. One such invitation was to join the photography course. It was a marvellous experience, during the display in City Hall, to see how our society was seen through the eyes of someone who was new to our country and our city. It was also so important for the young people to relate to someone who might otherwise have appeared as a threat. Such integration creates social solidarity among people.

Work and human dignity
In *DORAS Luimní* such social solidarity and integration is encouraged and developed through voluntary work engaged in by people in the asylum process. *Work is the Key* as the Bishops so aptly titled their document on the importance of work to our sense of self and to the necessity of contributing to society. For people in the asylum process to work is a criminal offence, so they cannot contribute to society in this way nor can they earn a living. The only way they can work is as volunteers. Many organisations like the St Vincent De Paul, sports clubs and Civil Defence offer excellent opportunities for people to be occupied even if unable to be remunerated with money. The churches are

also an excellent source of voluntary occupation. Through these activities people's dignity is respected, they are occupied rather than bored, they are meeting people, their language skills are improving and they are contributing a valuable service to the community. One extremely negative effect of not earning money is people's purchasing power is zero. This means the social aspect of shopping is missing. When people stand in queues they are visible. Removing this aspect of their lives makes them invisible and mysterious and, in many cases, contributes to their extreme isolation and ghettoisation. These divisions do not contribute to a healthy society.

The following story illustrates this point about work and the value of work and how it contributes to our mental, spiritual and physical well-being. Among the people in Limerick at one time was a carpenter. The Vincent De Paul Society accepted him to mend furniture in their store-house. He got about five other people as his helpers, trained them, and together they offered a very good service. It was mutually beneficial to all and went on for some time. This was excellent in terms of implementing the gospel, the social teaching of the church, and Christian charity. But of course, what happened? The head carpenter was moved to Dublin. With this move not only did Vincent de Paul lose a very good service, but this man lost what had given him a huge sense of self worth and dignity, plus all his network of friends and supports. This is just one example of how the state system can work against the social teaching and gospel principles. It also leaves us with a challenge as to how we continue to ensure that human dignity is respected, and vulnerable people are supported and developed in this limbo stage of existence.

Refugee status and the right to work
When people get recognition of their refugee status, they have the right to work, own property etc. In other words, they have all the rights of an Irish national to live life in a normal way, except the right to vote in national and presidential elections. We often find that they find it difficult to enter the work force and

get a fair wage. The social teaching in documents such as *Gaudium et Spes*, (1965) *Justice in the World*, (1971) and *Laborem Exercens*, (John Paul II, 1981) puts forward some principles on proper treatment of workers with some mentioning of the rights of refugees and migrant workers. Often people who get refugee status are so fearful that they accept inhumane and unjust situations at work. In *DORAS*, we keep in touch with people who have refugee status, and we published a short booklet, *Information for Refugees*, which is given to each person to enable them to navigate this stage of their turbulent lives. We also encourage them to join SIPTU, or whichever trade union is most appropriate to their situation. Again we see the importance of collaborating with such agents as the Trade Union movement in forwarding and achieving the ideals of Catholic social teaching. Our aim is to ensure that people's dignity is respected, and that people have access to fair treatment in the workplace. Many of these people have been terrified and silenced for so long and been victims of unjust systems, we have a duty to enable them to regain their voices. Because some of these people are vulnerable to being caught in unjust systems, structures and institutions, we need to be on the alert in ensuring that these factors do not contribute to unjust work practices and conditions developing and becoming acceptable in our society. This is put very strongly in *Justice in the World* and the strong message of *Laborem Exercens* is that nobody who is in another country should be exploited.

The value of a person's work should be measured according to objective standards and not determined by the colour of a person's skin, race, nationality, religion, political or social grouping. This is also the ideal of the Equality Authority here in Ireland, so again we need to use the tools and institutions of secular society to give the legal backing we need to achieve the aims of Catholic social teaching – a just and equitable society for all where people's dignity and rights are respected.

Solidarity and fellowship – challenges for today
The aspects that challenge us all today, as I see it, are solidarity

and fellowship – the cornerstones of Christianity. This means standing beside those who are excluded, victimised, voiceless in our society, remembering that this happens because society (us) organises itself in ways that create exclusion. It is a huge challenge to us to even look at our social, economic, political and cultural organisation and see how we have organised them in such a way as to exclude people, or to say it is alright to prohibit a certain group of people from earning a living. How do we create fellowship among us and between us when our society is structured in such a way as to segregate and exclude? Our call to celebrate this solidarity and fellowship in eucharist is indeed a challenge.

There are so many aspects of the life of people seeking asylum, the response of *DORAS Luimní* and its interface with Catholic social teaching that I could explore and expand on, but perhaps I will finish with yet another story. As I walked along the streets of Dublin one day in late November 2003, I was unexpectedly greeted with joy and acknowledgement. The greeting came from a person who had lived in one of the hostels in Limerick while his application for refugee status was being processed. After his claim was recognised he moved to Dublin. He insisted on bringing me for coffee. It was Ramadan. He would not take even a cup of water but insisted on a coffee for me. We talked and talked. In the course of the conversation he said that the one remarkable aspect of *DORAS* was that everyone was welcomed irrespective of nationality, colour, creed. He said that people in the hostels learned from the example of *DORAS* how to tolerate each other, even though in their home countries they would have found this very difficult. The inspiration for this approach can certainly be found in the documents from Vatican II, the Ecumenical Council – a prolonged social teaching event. This concept is the inspiration for how to treat the stranger and develop a Christian response in a rapidly changing world.

Catholic social teaching has so much to offer us if we allow it to come into dialogue with the issues of our time and if we explore them from this perspective. It has so much to offer such groups as *DORAS Luimní* in enabling us to respond while being involved in the political issues. It challenges us to progress Christian charity and the work for just structures, enabling all people to live in dignity in societies that respect and protect their rights irrespective of the outside political and economic forces. As Christians we are called to show solidarity with those excluded and on the margins. Catholic social teaching should create this awareness in us and inspire us to respond. As Pope John Paul II puts it in *Centesimus Annus:*

> Love of others and in the first place love for the poor, in whom the church sees Christ himself, is made concrete in the promotion of justice.

CHAPTER SEVEN

Action for Justice

Ronan Barry

Coming down to practical and particularly urgent consequences, this council lays stress on reverence for man; everyone must consider his every neighbour without exception as another self, taking into account first of all his life and the means necessary to living it with dignity,[8] so as not to imitate the rich man who had no concern for the poor man Lazarus.[9]
In our times a special obligation binds us to make ourselves the neighbour of every person without exception, and of actively helping him when he comes across our path, whether he be an old person abandoned by all, a foreign labourer unjustly looked down upon, a refugee, a child born of an unlawful union and wrongly suffering for a sin he did not commit, or a hungry person who disturbs our conscience by recalling the voice of the Lord, 'As long as you did it for one of these the least of my brethren, you did it for me' (Mt 25:40).
Gaudium et Spes, Pastoral Constitution on the Church in the Modern World, Second Vatican Council, 1965

Catholic social teaching has never been a topical subject in the world of current affairs or with religious correspondents. However, numbers attending church liturgies, the numbers for first holy communion and confirmation, are often the topic of debate. Statistics are the criteria of success and failure in today's world. For today's media such statistics are considered sufficient to convey the depth of faith and belief of the people of God. Social teaching and social justice are criteria that can be used to look at the communities and their efforts to build the kingdom of God. The reason for the church's decision to be involved in social policy and social justice is clear, as it is teaching visibly embedded in the gospel. Catholic social teaching, such as that cited from *Gaudium et Spes*, clearly indicates the essential link between faith and justice, a link that must be made real in today's world.

> When I give food to the poor, they call me a saint. When I ask why the poor have no food, they call me a communist.
> — *Dom Helda Camara*

Is faith real without action? Can the Christian vision of social justice exist if it is not embedded in spirituality? It is my belief that justice and spirituality are intertwined, yet there is room for each subject to be researched, developed and experienced for the individual and the community we call society. Christian spirituality involves a call from God to be a witness to God's kingdom in his/her created world – a kingdom that has peace and inclusiveness, service and generosity at its centre.

This short essay, or personal commentary, is about my understanding of the links between faith and justice and the inseparability of both, as well as some questions I have that remain unanswered. The essay will also point to why, in some way, I am doing the work I do at present and it being central to restoring the link in a real, visible manner between justice and faith.

Like many a young person growing up I was involved in many discussions (as young people still are today) about God and if there is a God. Among the questions for me were: How could God allow the starvation of a country like Ethiopia? Why was there need for Live Aid (13 June 1985)? Why do young people die of cancer? Where was the God of Love, the God that was called 'Emmanuel'? These questions shaped me and focused my search for meaning in life. My search involved studying and investigating belief through academic study, including theology.

I studied theology with the hope that it would help me to deepen my understanding of God and the role of the Catholic Church and other churches as witnesses to Christianity. It turned out to be an academic exercise that had exams and results, but within this exercise I found little or no connection to the reality of everyday life. Theology helped me to think logically about issues of morality, dogma, heresies etc, but it failed to ignite in me any thrust to search and understand God, and God within my life, and God outside my life. It was in my study of theology that I heard for the first time about Catholic social teaching, but my sense was that it was something outside the real theology. Why that is the case I am not too sure. Was it how I heard it? Or was is the way it was taught?

After Theology, I spent time working with young adults, and some not so young, developing links between people and professional services as well as providing a confidential information service. This started to open my eyes to a reality that was far from the academic language of theology but was full of a new reality. This reality was hopeful and painful at the same time, a reality seeking certainty and security. In this reality there was a real search for meaning in life but in many different ways. It was this involvement with people's personal searches that pointed me to Emmanuel, 'God is with us'. This work, at the same time, pointed me inward to my own personal search and to a deeper understanding of God in my life. It challenged me to articulate my beliefs in a language that people could understand, a language that invited people to explore this spiritual aspect of life. This was a language that spoke of such issues as the pressure of meeting bills, of unplanned pregnancy, as well as allowing people to express doubts in God and the kingdom of God. It was a language that I found to be hopeful, generous, and God-giving.

People had clear questions about the meaning of life and God in their life. It was important to allow the person to be involved in a process which was dignified, a process that had listening and not necessarily answering, at its centre. In some way this two-way process allowed God, God who is Love, to be revealed, and the young person to find their peace in their own heart and mind. This was a time of great importance, of realising that faith that is not shared is not alive, and faith without work is not a witness to the real message of Christ. During this time there were still many people of faith who disparaged this work as second-rate compared to filling the pews on a Sunday. For some people the relationship with God is of a vertical nature with no horizontal axis, therefore they view this work as purely secular and not related to the work of the Kingdom.

As my career took a new path I started to work with young people. These young people were new to me, and they were young people whose circumstances and experiences were very different from the experience I had of being young, or that of any of my friends. It was difficult then for me to understand them, because a significant part of their experience had been dominated by aggression, by uncontrollable anger, and along with this they had substantial developmental needs. This experience was difficult for me, and in the beginning there were clear questions such as: How was I in all this? Where do you find God in all things? The questions allowed me to open myself up to many areas that were outside my comfort zone. These areas opened me to new understandings of other people's experiences. Listening to the stories of these young people allowed me to understand why someone might become so aggressive. Of course understanding it didn't excuse such behaviour, but I was challenged by it. What was I actually doing to help them? I know that I was reasonable in my work practices but, outside of work, was I involved in creating opportunities that would allow these young people to become more included in our society and our church? These questions continue to be valid to this day and will be valid for tomorrow.

I was fortunate to have had the opportunity to be part of the lives of these young people. The following example illustrates the kinds of questions I believe we should be concerned with.

One young person I worked with was a 15 year old young man, Tim, (not his real name), who was in trouble with the law since he was nine. I worked with Tim for about six months. He looked after me in the same way he looked after his younger siblings. He took it upon himself to show me the ropes of my new job; important things like how to avoid trouble with other young people, how to be fair, how to sit and relax with young people whom society labels as dangerous and out of control. These young people read newspapers and watch television where they read very clearly that society (us) wants them locked up and the key thrown away; and you can imagine how that makes them feel. It certainly doesn't help them to feel included. It achieves the opposite and further alienates them within our society.

When Tim was told by the courts that he was allowed to leave the care of the state, he did so. Like many others, Tim left without any real support as his parents were not at home. He had no place to sleep, so he slept on the street. He had no money, so he robbed. And the vicious circle started again, and will continue until one day when he may be lucky enough to get the right judge, the right probation officer and the right set of circumstances.

Some years later, I worked with Tim's younger brother Cian, (not his real name), another young person struggling with substantial needs, which were further complicated by addiction.

Cian was another young person whom society could not keep safe, another young person we eventually excluded, even with all the interventions of the state. This young person eventually believed that the state and its system of intervention was the enemy. Cian, like Tim, went through the revolving door in the social service system. He was placed and replaced in residential care, and ran away and was placed again, until he got too old for the system. Some years later Cian approached another service-user organisation for help. He had been living on the streets beside one of Dublin's largest shopping centres. He came looking for help because he was charged with stealing a sleeping bag, and was worried about being locked up again. Cian had many developmental problems that still needed attention. He could neither read nor write, but it seemed that he would have to sort these problems out in prison. I always wondered, if Tim and Cian had been given the appropriate settings to address their needs, where they would be now. Tim is now serving time in prison in another country.

These young people posed many questions for me which I believe are relevant to us all. Have we helped them to experience something of the kingdom of God, of justice, peace and love, now, on earth? Or are they to be alienated from the kingdom on earth by experiencing only its opposite?

We are asked by our Christian faith to reach out to others and there are many ways to do this. Generally, most of us have been lucky enough to experience right relationships with our peers, our families, our God, and we are now called to reach out to others in need, who have not experienced right relationship. We are called to work with all for the kingdom, with inclusiveness and peace at its centre ... your kingdom come, your will be done on earth as it is in heaven ... (Mt).

> Justice is a harmony that comes from fidelity to right relationships with God, people, institutions and the environment.
> *CORI Justice Commission*

The issue of social justice asks many questions of ourselves and our response to issues in today's world, and leads to personal questions about who and what sustains us in the long term. This desire for social justice calls us to deepen our spirituality to listen to God more closely about how to build up God's kingdom now.

For some people, praying, spending time with our God, is one way of doing this. Others will say it is a waste of time when you could be doing something more useful (something I might have said when I was younger). However, praying allows God to work through us. It is during this time that we can become aware of what God's love for us really means. God's call to us is to bring people into good relationship with each other, with the community where they live, and with God. It is God's sustaining love that we discover in prayer, that allows us the energy and the focus to help create his kingdom, where there is justice and peace, inclusiveness and participation, a kingdom without alienation or marginalisation. In John's gospel we hear Jesus say, 'I have come that they may have life, and have it to the full' (John10:10). For the followers of Jesus, this is the call for social justice for all here and now. This call to be active for justice has many expressions in the social teaching of the church. A clear instance is in the document *Justice in the World,* of the 1971 Synod of Bishops, and repeated in the Irish Bishops' Pastoral of 1977, *The Work of Justice.*

> Action on behalf of justice and participation in the transformation of the world appear to us as a constitutive dimension of the preaching of the gospel.
> Christian love of neighbour and justice cannot be separated. For love implies an absolute demand for justice, namely a recognition of the dignity and rights of one's neighbour. Justice attains its inner fullness only in love ... (p 19).

It has been my experience that the church has failed to claim the work of social justice. There is a sense at times that there is no link between having a relationship with God and social justice. I believe you can't have one without the other, that a justice without spirituality is a service without love. The government of today presents many services to many disadvantaged people but many are still excluded. Christian teaching on social justice constantly asks us to include all, to allow all to participate in our society.

The work I am presently engaged in is about providing experiential opportunities to explore faith and justice with young adults. It involves working with full and part-time volunteers. It is about creating and re-creating the links between justice and spirituality. Generally young adults believe in justice. However, sometimes they see it as having no real link to spirituality.

The work of *Slí Eile Volunteer Communities* is about giving opportunities to young adults to face challenging issues in our society. These social justice issues help them to explore areas where society has failed to include people, and to look at a society, which accepts exclusion. While being full-time volunteers for one year in services working with people and groups on the edge of society, the volunteers also take time to explore their own personal beliefs in regard to faith and justice. Volunteers relate their experience as discovering a God who includes all people, a God who is calling all people to build his kingdom now, to be involved in the work of justice. Volunteers at the end of this year convey the experience as beginning a new journey in life with treasures revealed.

Sometimes for us the challenge as individuals to get involved is too big, especially if we know that it could change us profoundly. You hear people say 'No, I couldn't do that. I would get too caught up in it', or 'How do you do that? It must be difficult to see that every day.' This is a real concern for many people as it is seen as an individual calling, or something they have to do on their own. That is why it is important to remind ourselves that we are all called together to do this work as a community of God. It is in doing it together we can realise the full extent of God working through us. It is in the challenge of the work, the sharing of the experience of the work, with each other, and the sharing of our time and gifts with people, that important questions arise. Who is God in our lives? Why are people in our society allowed to suffer like that? It is together we will find answers, it is together we will enhance our understanding of life, and it is together we will deepen our spirituality.

The text from *Gaudium et Spes* at the start of the essay points to the urgency of considering everyone as your neighbour, of treating people with respect and dignity. This challenge is monumental and needs to be taken up each day. The church as well as society can point to various failings where the call to social justice was intentionally ignored for the sake of 'peace' or 'politics'. However if we, fail to take up this call again and again we are failing our very own faith, our Christian spirituality. The link between justice and spirituality is strong and alive; it may have been forgotten or hidden, but if rediscovered and renewed by communities and church alike it will give a new voice which speaks clearly and loudly for those who have none, but more importantly it will give the excluded a voice.

Faith Without Works is Dead
What good is it, my brothers, if a man claims to have faith but has no deeds? Can such faith save him? Suppose a brother or sister is without clothes and daily food. If one of you says to him, 'Go, I wish you well; keep warm and well fed,' but does nothing about his physical needs, what good is it? In the same way, faith by itself, if it is not accompanied by action, is dead. But someone will say, 'You have faith; I have deeds.' Show me your faith without deeds, and I will show you my faith by what I do. You believe that there is one God. Good! Even the demons believe that – and shudder. You foolish man. Do you want evidence that faith without deeds is useless? Was not our ancestor Abraham considered righteous for what he did when he offered his son Isaac on the altar? You see that his faith and his actions were working together, and his faith was made complete by what he did. And the scripture was fulfilled that says, 'Abraham believed God, and it was credited to him as righteousness,' and he was called God's friend. You see that a person is justified by what he does and not by faith alone. In the same way, was not even Rahab the prostitute considered righteous for what she did when she gave lodging to the spies and sent them off in a different direction? As the body without the spirit is dead, so faith without deeds is dead.' *(Jas 2:14-26)*

CHAPTER EIGHT

Catholic Social Teaching: Opening the Chest

Susan Jones CHF

Introduction
The social teaching of the Catholic Church is like a dark treasure chest filled with many strings of pearls and precious jewels. Unlike the treasure buried in a field it is there for all to benefit from what it holds, but for various reasons few have ventured to unpack it. Upon opening the chest one could be dazzled by the brilliance and boldness of it, and may suddenly slam the lid shut again for its dazzling light might illuminate more than we wish to see. For those who dip in and pick up the jewels it soon becomes clear that no chain is separate, they are interlinked. In many ways it is difficult to appreciate one jewel without the rest. The church's social teaching has evolved over time with each encyclical developing from the previous one in some way. And with each new encyclical comes the feeling that the church is continuing to develop its own understanding of its mission to humanity, one of lengthy service.[1]

If our church is rooted in the gospel and founded on Jesus Christ, one is left with a question, why do we need social teaching in the first place? I believe we need it as it helps us to unpack the message of the gospel in light of our ever changing world and the various global crises that have arisen in history down to the present day. It calls us back to a more authentic discipleship of Jesus rather than a devotional following of him. We are left in no doubt that the teaching is no longer the sole responsibility of the magisterium but that its success is dependent on all

---

1. John Paul II, *Redemptor Hominis* (London: Catholic Truth Society, 1979), #21.

Catholics and people of good will.² Following Jesus' example, this discipleship demands that we walk in his sandals among people of today and enable all to develop to their full humanity. The call to enable all to reach their potential as children of God, and to recognise their worth as human beings is intrinsic to the mission of the church and at the heart of the church's social teaching.³ It must begin by enabling people to recognise their worth as human beings. This I see as the thread that binds all the jewels in the treasure chest of the church's social teaching together, and this fills me with great hope.

Why is the vocation and dignity of the human person essential to the church's social teaching?

If the vocation and dignity of the human person were not at the core of the church's social teaching something fundamental would be missing in how it approaches the needs of people. The church may find itself guilty of some of the sin it seeks to convert individuals and nations from. John XXIII helped to answer this question when he said, 'They [human beings] are by grace the children and friends of God and heirs to eternal glory.'⁴ They are raised to a dignity through the life, death and resurrection of Jesus. It is through the incarnation that Jesus united himself with humanity to help humans understand their divine calling.⁵ This was at the heart of that wonderful document of Vatican II, *Gaudium et Spes*, 'For by his power to know himself in the depths of his being he rises above the whole universe of mere objects. When he is drawn to think about his real self he turns to those deep recesses of his being where God who probes the heart awaits him, and where he himself decides his own destiny in the

---

2. Austin Flannery, *Vatican Council II* (Dublin: Dominican Publications,1975), *Gaudium et Spes* #2.
3. Paul VI, *Populorum Progressio* (London: Catholic Truth Society, 1968), #13-15.
4. Gremillion, J., *The Gospel of Peace and Justice* (New York: Orbis Books, 1976), John XXIII *Pacem in Terris* #10.
5. *RH* #18.

sight of God.'[6] *(Quotes taken directly from encyclicals and church documents are not in inclusive language.)* Where does this power to know ourselves come from? It is Christ who reveals humanity to itself, and helps us understand our vocation,[7] and it is through his divinity that our final goal becomes attainable?[8] Ultimately our human destiny, our vocation is divine. We have been created for our own sake[9] and we are created to give God glory. We have been redeemed by God, reconciled to him through Jesus.[10] As St Paul reminds us, we are a new creation through the gift of Jesus.[11] We are justified, made righteous.[12] Our alienation from God is transformed, and we have a way to reach our true end with God.[13] It was an act of love which put humanity back in right relationship with God. It is then the mission of the church to tell all people of their intrinsic value and dignity.[14]

---

6. *GS* #14. Also see *GS* #22.
7. *RH* #8.
8. *Catechism of the Catholic Church* (Dublin: Veritas, 1983), #1700. The Catechism tells us that 'the dignity of the human person is rooted in his creation in the image and likeness of God; it is fulfilled in his vocation to divine beatitude. It is essential to the human dignity freely to direct himself to this fulfilment.' The ultimate fulfilment is the kingdom and a sharing in the divine.
9. *GS* #14 and #2.
10. 2 Cor 5:18-19.
11. The writings of St Paul to the Galatians and the Romans expand on this redeeming act of making us a new creation. We are invited to embrace this new creation, to put on Christ. As humans we are called to partake in the now and also to wait hopefully for the kingdom to come.
12. 2 Cor 5:21.
13. The 'kind of justice God does in Christ transforms persons at the level of being'. Haughey, J. C., 'Jesus as the Justice of God' in Haughey, J. C., (ed.), *The Faith That Does Justice* (New York: Paulist Press, 1977), pp 264-289, p 283.
14. *RH* #12 This also affirms the teaching on Religious Liberty in *Dignitas Humane* #2 where the church recognised all people's right to seek the truth. 'It is in accordance with their dignity that all men, because they are persons, that is, being endowed with reason and free will and therefore bearing personal responsibility, are both impelled by their nature and bound by a moral obligation to seek the truth, especially religious truth.'

OPENING THE CHEST

How do human beings know of their vocation? Where does that sense of their life's mission come from?

What sets humans apart, as we know, is our ability to think and reason. From the core of our being and aided by our conscience, we have the ability to reflect on our life, to grow in relation to ourselves and others, and to shape our environment. Paul VI tells the church that 'Man as an individual and as a member of society craves a life that is full, autonomous and worthy of his nature as a human being; he longs to harness for his own welfare the immense resources of the modern world.'[15] It is from deep within that we respond to God's plan, that we follow a law that comes with the nature of being human. Natural Law,[16] which is well established in the early social teaching of the church, is quite controversial. But it suffices here to say that there exists some sort of law that lies within humanity. This law exists despite race, creed or gender. St Paul acknowledged it when he said that even the pagans who have never been taught the law follow it.[17] This law is 'concerned with the rational direction of human life towards ends human beings can understand as worthwhile. And these ends themselves are not arbitrary, but are part of the overall end of things to which God lovingly and wisely directs the entire universe.'[18] We need to tune into our Creator God's plan for our salvation, so that we can know how to use the gifts and skills we were born with for our own fulfilment and the good of the world.[19]

Why link human vocation and dignity?

In his opening address to the 3rd CELAM gathering in Puebla on 28 January 1979 John Paul II quoted a line from his Christmas

---
15. *GS* #9.
16. According to Thomas Aquinas human being's participation in the Eternal Law of God is Natural Law. Thos Aquinas, *S. Th.* 1-11,q.1; a-1; q. 93.9.1-2.
17. Rom 2:14.
18. Komonchak, J. A., Collins, M., Lane, D. A., *The New Dictionary of Theology* (Minnesota: The Liturgical Press, 1987), pp 706-707. This aspect is addressed in *GS* #16.
19. *PP* #15.

address of 1978. He said, 'the human being is single, unique and unrepeatable, someone thought of and chosen from eternity, someone called and identified by name.'[20] There is only one of every person in the world and each person only gets one chance to live their life. No matter how much charity and compassion we have for another we cannot live their lives for them. To use a much quoted Hassidic legend, 'Before his death Rabbi Sussja said: "in the world to come, I will not be asked, 'Why were you not Moses?' I will be asked, 'Why were you not Sussja?'"'[21] What becomes essential for each person to live their vocation is a sense of their own dignity and a confidence in their worth as a person.[22] People have to be treated in such a way as to respect their human dignity. Thus there is an objective and subjective human dignity. The former aspect of human dignity makes use of the Kantian notion of respect owed to a person because they are human. It is this understanding that gives rise to the concept of rights to which I shall return. The latter refers to our own sense of our dignity.[23]

However, there is a very important distinction to be made between a subjective and an objective human dignity. Aurel Kolnai says that 'Human Dignity', (objective human dignity) is threatened mainly by the impact on us of powers alien to our own will, whereas our lack of 'dignity as a quality' (subjective human dignity), or indeed our indignity is mainly our own work; it can express itself or come to be expected through our own agency.[24] A point made by Paul VI in *Populorum Progressio*

---

20. Charles, R., & Maclearn, D., *The Social Teaching of Vatican II* (San Francisco: Ignatius Press, 1982), p 470.
21. Kelly K., quoting from Josef Fuch's 'Christian Morality: The Word Becomes Flesh' (Dublin: Gill & Macmillan, 1987) p 143 in *New Directions in Moral Theology* (London: Geoffrey Chapman, 1992), p 31.
22. See Hill, T. E., 'Servility and Self Respect' in Dillon, R. S., (ed.), *Dignity, Character and Self Respect* (New York: Routledge, 1995), p 76-92.
23. I believe that this is the understanding that is reflected more heavily in the early Church's Social Teaching which seemed to emphasise what humanity needed in the external forums, eg. The condition of labour in *Rerum Novarum*, the rights to property, the right to economic progress in Pius XI's *Quadragesimo Anno*, etc.
24. Aurel Kolnai 'Dignity' in Dillon, R. S., (ed.), *Dignity, Character & Self*

expresses that we may or may not achieve our intended destiny: 'Endowed with intelligence and freedom, he is responsible for his fulfillment as he is for his salvation. He is aided, or sometimes impeded, by those who educate him and those with whom he lives, but each one remains, whatever be the influences affecting him, the principal agent of his own success or failure.'[25]

The subjective sense of human dignity, our own self-respect is intriguing. J. C. Haughey has a wonderful commentary on the Beatitudes (Mt 5:3-10) which I believe helps to clarify our understanding of human dignity in a way which is reflected in the church's social teaching more strongly from Vatican II on. Verse 6 reads, 'Happy are those who hunger and thirst for what is right, they shall be satisfied.' Haughey says, 'that the primary meaning of righteousness cannot be ethical conduct since the hearers are described as being in quest for this quality rather than capable of bringing it about through their own efforts in the present order of things.'[26] His comments on verse 10, clarifies things a little more. 'Happy are those who are persecuted in the cause of right; theirs is the kingdom of heaven.' Here he maintains that we are aware something is missing which we hunger for so we try to attain it. We know by our lack of dignity at a deeper level that we are destined for better, so we risk persecution to get our dignity. This striving for dignity in itself gives us dignity.[27] In the last beatitude 'Happy are you when people abuse you and persecute you and speak all kinds of calumny against you on my account. Rejoice for your reward will be great

---

Respect, op. cit. pp 53-75. First published in 'Philosophy' 5 1976, Royal Institute of Philosophy. Kolnai gives a good example to illustrate the fact that aspects of the dignity given to us can be suppressed or taken away e.g. our right to education, right to cultural expression etc., but they may not always take away our sense of our own dignity but other activities may destroy our dignity because we ourselves are restricted in being allowed to shape our lives.
25. *PP* #15
26. Haughey, J.C., op. cit. p 276.
27. See Dillon. R. S., 'Introduction' in, *Dignity, Character & Self Respect* op. cit. p 24.

in heaven' (v 11). Here the person fighting for dignity is the one fighting for Jesus as the fullness of dignity as image of God, revealed.[28] Our vocation and our dignity go together in Jesus Christ. 'The worth and dignity of every human person is expressed in creation and confirmed in the incarnation and redemption.'[29] According to John Paul it is the whole person the church must serve, helping him/her to realise how much they are loved by God and how much God desires that they find their way to Godself.[30]

How is the church's mission to the dignity of humanity reflected in its social teaching?

If the church is to ensure the whole person's development it has to enable the human person also to develop themselves, for we are co-creators with God. Our call to the transcendent is always a call to transcend ourselves. What we find echoed in many documents is the necessity for humanity to play a role in shaping their own lives, communities, countries etc. While much of the social teaching recognises that it should be those on top who help those whose dignity is destroyed as a result of generations of unjust treatment, the church also invites all people to work for their own dignity, especially the poor.[31] The latter group may be given all the objective dignity a person deserves. However this will only empower them as people if they can find the grace within to acknowledge their own worth.[32] The Pope says, 'God

---

28. Haughey J. C., op. cit. p. 277.
29. McDonagh, E. 'Redemptor Hominis and Ireland' in *The Furrow* (1979), vol 30, pp 625-640, p 635.
30. *RH* #13.
31. Paul addressed this in *Octogesima Advenians* with recognising that the movement into urban areas and industry has brought new problems for humanity and that they need to find a way to get involved in decision-making. See #48. Yet according to the 1971 Synod on Justice in the World, it is not the church's mission as an ecclesiastical hierarchal community to come up with ways of doing this. The church calls on it's members to be a leaven in society and influence it according to Christian values. See #37-38.
32. See Dorr, D., *Spirituality and Justice* (Dublin: Gill & Macmillan, 1984), p 79.

grant that there may be many of us to offer you unselfish co-operation in order that you may free yourselves from everything that in a certain way enslaves you, but with full respect for what you are and for your right to be the prime authors of your human advancement.'[33] While outlining the aspirations of humanity in *Populorum Progressio* and the importance of education in enabling people to take responsibility for their lives,[34] Pope Paul also notes the fact that as a result of economic growth many of our poor have 'almost no possibility of acting responsibly and on their own initiative'.[35] It is this that underpins the whole need for radical changes in society. The 1971 Synod on Justice tried to address this concern by demanding that the social structures, which prevent people from developing be removed.[36] The poor must have a say in shaping their lives especially in the area of politics. According to Paul VI, this shaping of life goes beyond acquiring material things and services, to ensuring that people have access to all that a person needs to fulfill their vocation. For him all human activity must be according to God's will so that people will be able to live a fully human life.[37]

Kevin Kelly, in describing the dignity of the human person, draws on Louis Janssen's *Eight Fundamental Dimensions of the Human Person*, four of which I would like to use to explore the church's social teaching.[38] The first is that (a) *the human person is embodied*. In Leo XIII's *Rerumn Novarum* one might think that

---

33. See Dorr, D., *Option for the Poor* (Dublin: Gill & Macmillan, 1983), p 229 where he quotes The Pope John Paul II speaking to people living in the shanty town of Favela dos Alagados in Brazil. Taken from *L'Obsservor Romano* 4 August, 1981 p 7.
34. *PP* #35. In addressing the issue of education in the 1971 Synodal Document, the bishops maintain in developing countries the principal aim of education for justice consists in an 'attempt to awaken consciences to a knowledge of the concrete situation and in a call to secure a total improvement'. Synod of Bishops 1971, *Justice in the World* (Athlone: St Pauls Publications, 1971), #51.
35. *PP* #9. Also see #65.
36. *Justice in the World* #16.
37. *GS* #35.
38. Kevin, K., op. cit. p 30, quoting from Louis Janssen's article 'Artificial Insemination; ethical considerations', *Louvain Studies*, 1980 pp 3-39.

there is a dualistic approach to the human person for he says, 'it is the soul which is made after the image and likeness of God'.[39] It is to the soul that he attributes all equality as humans and because of this they should be treated equally. It was from this position that the church defended the dignity and rights of workers because they are God's.[40] Our understanding of the concepts in this foundational document has evolved with the advances of human psychology and self-understanding. Today the church recognises that human beings must be cared for in their totality and that as embodied beings we are called to live out the fullness of our humanity in a materialist world.[41] As embodied beings we are affected by all that living in this world entails and we can be empowered or diminished by advances in society and the world of trade and economics.[42] John Paul II warns that humanity needs to be careful not to end up being manipulated or enslaved by the materialistic society it is creating.[43] 'The church cannot remain insensitive to whatever serves man's true welfare',[44] for human destiny is 'so closely and unbreakably linked with Christ'.[45] The church must continue to safeguard the freedom, which is vital for human development, both external and internal.

(b) *Human beings are equal.* In his ministry on earth Jesus went to the sick, the disabled, the women and children, (Lk 8:40-56, Mt 8:1-4) the outcasts, the foreigners (Mk 7:24-30), the stranger (Mt 8:5-13) and the searcher (Jn 3:1-21). In doing so through word and act he restored their dignity as children of God. All people were treated equally. The church, while still seeking to fulfill its mission, puts before the world the message that 'All men are endowed with a rational soul and are created in God's image; they have the same nature and origin and, being re-

---

39. Leo XIII, *Rerum Novarum* #40 [on-line]
40. *RN* #41ff.
41. Austin Flannary, op. cit., *Lumen Gentium* , #18.
42. *PP* #20-21.
43. *RH* #16.
44. *RH* #13.
45. *RH* #14.

deemed by Christ, they enjoy the same divine calling and destiny; there is a basic equality between all men and it must be given greater recognition.[46] As human beings we all share rights, born out of human dignity. Pope John XXIII clearly outlined these rights in a comprehensive way in his encyclical *Pacem in Terris*.[47] But he went a step further; he added the fact that we have duties.[48] As human beings each of us has the duty to take up our responsibility and use the rights given us for our fulfilment. Yet we also have to embrace the church's teaching and ensure that we give to others their rights and treat them with the dignity they are due as people. When we are treated with dignity we know ourselves to be of value and this external reality nurtures our internal sense of self-respect and subjective dignity. Above all it enables us to appreciate the value of the other and see their uniqueness. Kelly explains that our uniqueness is further enhanced by how we network and are affected by others.[49] This is important in relation to the building of community.

(c) Human beings are inter-relational. As we grow up we become aware of the separateness of others, that we have a life of our own. However, the irony is that it is only from others that we begin to shape our identity as a person. Our human vocation is fundamentally linked to the rest of humanity. It is due to this connectedness of humanity as the Body of Christ that John Paul II urges people to follow a 'principle of solidarity'[50] which will guide economic change so that all people can develop equally. And he uses the judgement scene in Matthew's gospel to support this action for it recognises that Christ is equally present in all of us: 'Whatever you did for the least of my children, you did for me' (Mt 25:45). This building up of humanity requires that we use the gifts given to us as unique individuals for ourselves, and the good of our neighbour.

---

46. *GS* #29.
47. *PT* #11-27.
48. Ibid #28-38.
49. Kelly, K., op. cit., p 53.
50. *RH* #16; also see *PP* #48.

(d) *Human beings are interdependent.* This is reflected wholeheartedly in the social teaching in 'The Common Good'. This is 'the sum total of all those conditions of social life which enable individuals, families and organisations to achieve complete and effective fulfillment.'[51] The church continually puts before those responsible for economic development and for the running of society that the common good must at all times respect the individuals who live in a society and supply them with what they need to live with dignity and integrity.[52] John Paul II in *Sollicitudo Rei Socialis* reminds the people again that if a member of the Body of Christ is denied the opportunity to attain fulfilment the whole body is held back.[53] This is a present day reality as the gap between rich and poor widens within countries as well as internationally. Therefore it is vital for the good of all that the poor and powerless be enabled to contribute to their community in all its aspects as well as the state at large. Otherwise the destiny of humanity will never be fully attained.

So, why does the church's social teaching on the dignity of the human person strike me as important in what I have chosen to do?
How does the church's social teaching affect the daily life of a Catholic in the developed world? We may think that the social teaching is only geared towards those living in the developed world in relation to attitudes, policies, economic activity, regarding those in the developing world. This thinking would undermine the message of the gospel, for all are called to live the justice of God. 'The person is brought into the new creation and into the dynamism of the justice of God in order that justice might also be done through him and through the Body of Christ

---

51. *GS* #74, also see Kelly, K. op.cit., p 47, and *MM* #59-60.
52. e.g. John XXIII appeals to public authorities *MM* #54. In developing the teaching of *Rerum Novarum*, he makes it clear that at times states will have to intervene in the private economic sphere if people are being exploited, but at all times the person should never be denied the right to engage in enterprise or industry.
53. John Paul II, *Sollicitudo Rei Socialis* (Dublin: Veritas Publications, 1988), #38.

of which he has been made a member.'[54] We continue to create God's creation, for where human beings are, God will be transforming society in and through them.

It is good and essential that those in developed countries help those in developing countries but it can be truly more difficult to see and help the poor person at our doorstep, especially when we measure poverty only by the images presented to us of those experiencing famine and war. Yes we have a duty to use our knowledge and voice to enable and empower the poor to speak up, while working in solidarity with them to change systems and structures that are limiting their freedom and possibilities to live their vocation. There definitely needs to be a preferential option for the poor. But if the gospel message is for all and the call to live and act justly is addressed to all, how does it speak to people in the middle class? It goes without saying that people in this area are educated to some level, have adequate housing and some amount of disposable income. Most can choose to engage in society and contribute to the shaping of their environment if they wish. They are aware of their rights and most, I would say, experience themselves as treated with dignity. But I wonder, among this ever increasing section of society, with its heavy demands regarding working hours, status, and image, if there is a growing alienation from self and consequently from God, others and the justice call of the gospel?[55]

Do the concerns of John Paul II expressed in *Redemptor Hominis* hold true for some people whom society situates in the middle class?[56] For many, the freedom they need in order to know themselves and to know themselves as loved and redeemed by God is being eroded by the norms of society resulting from our social structures. Is there opportunity to nurture the quality of human dignity, that inner self worth (subjective dignity) so essential to living our life to the full? What people

---

54. Haughey, J. C., op.cit. p. 285.
55. *Justice in the World*, #50.
56. *RH* #15.

own and possess is becoming the measure of human worth. Yet acquiring more is not helping the human person to embrace all aspects of their vocation to divine happiness. I believe there are many who do not know how to listen and discern God's law written in their hearts, nor do they seem able to take the time. The emptiness this creates is being filled with a drivenness to have more. As equals in God's creation, God's justice extends to these people as well as to the poor. 'God accepts those who have no claim to be accepted; promises to make sense out of each individual's existence no matter how senseless it may seem, and values every human life however valueless others may regard it.'[57] John Paul recognises the fact that human systems don't give human beings true freedom and therefore the church has to be guardian of a freedom that is necessary for the dignity of the person.[58] So there is a need for the gospel message as embraced in the social teaching to be brought into the midst of this reality.[59]

How is the social teaching of the church and the need for evangelisation of the middle classes linked?
Love is the key and this love is Jesus. 'The man who wishes to understand himself thoroughly ... must, so to speak, enter into him [Jesus Christ] with all his own self, he must "appropriate" and assimilate the whole of the reality of the incarnation and redemption in order to find himself.'[60] It is at this level that a person will begin to wonder at him/herself and appreciate his/her true dignity. The gospel message in its fullness must be brought to the middle classes in a way that transcends the social structure in which they find themselves trapped, so they can know the depth of God's love for them as people. There is a need to nurture faith in God, to evangelise the middle class. The conver-

---

57. Komonchak, J. A., Collins, M., Lane, D. A., *The New Dictionary of Theology* op. cit., p 553.
58. *RH* #12.
59. Paul VI, *Evangelii Nuntiandi* (London: Catholic Truth Society, 1975) #29. This emphasises that the gospel has to be made relevant to the culture in which it is being proclaimed.
60. *RH* #10.

sion of one person has a ripple effect, which touches the family, the community and society. Therefore, how I relate in my ordinary living with the people with whom I work is vital. I must endeavor to treat everyone I encounter with the respect and dignity, not that they are due but that is already present in them as a child of God.[61] James Wallace says, 'that benevolence, kindness, generosity, and compassion are virtues – traits that "foster good human life in extensive and fundamental ways" – in large because the expression of them supports the self respect of their recipients by affirming their intrinsic worth and importance as person.'[62] I must also try to enable people to take time to appreciate their life in a deeper way. Faith helps people to accept that which is beyond limited human knowing. It enables all as beings created in God's image and likeness and loved by God to engage in relationship with this truth. God wants what is good for all people so he/she invites all to respond to his/her purpose for their life.[63] Our vocation is life.

Faith and justice are inseparable. We cannot love God and not serve our neighbour. The implication is that all have to work for justice. For those in the middle classes it is essential that they too are educated in the justice call of the gospel.[64] They must be helped to reflect on society and how they live. They too must try to renounce ways of living and doing business that are unjust or disempower others.[65] They must be helped to embrace a life stance of justice.[66] How people live today shapes tomorrow and the future of the next generation.

---

61. See *Justice in the World* #49
62. See Dillon, R. S., quoting from Wallace, J., *Virtues and Vice* (Ithaca: Cornell University Press, 1978), pp 152-158, op.cit., p 24.
63. See Maly, E. H., *Romans* (Dublin: Veritas Publications, 1979), p 69.
64. As the Synod of 1971 reminds us all, 'Action on behalf of justice and participation in the transformation of the world fully appear to us as a constitutive dimension of the preaching of the gospel.' #6.
65. See *Justice in the World* #51.
66. See Gaffney, J., 'On The Need Of Faith For Justice' in Gene, J., (ed.), *The Search For Faith And Justice In The Twenth Century* (New York: Paragon House Publishers, 1987), p 141.

Summary

At the heart of the church's social teaching is the human person, not just as a being who can do and create, but the human person who is created in the image and likeness of God and redeemed by Jesus Christ. The truth of this lies within every person as they seek to be their true self. In order to attain this end, their life's vocation, they must know themselves to be of worth and also experience themselves as being worthy of dignity and respect. While we can afford others this respect and dignity, it is the inner sense of dignity that is fundamentally important. This aspect of our being lies within the person's control to a large extent. Every person is obliged to grow in understanding their own worth, and to take responsibility for living their own life in their situation despite the action of others. (This is not condoning the immoral actions or unjust treatment of people towards each other.) In the living of our human lives we must see that all human beings are equal in being while external forces may say otherwise. This basic human equality is what draws us into responsibility to our neighbour for we are inter-related to them as persons and interdependent on them to attain our end. In Christ we all make up his body so we have to nurture the life of this body, especially the weaker parts. But within this body there is a new illness taking hold. It is not clearly evident but it is there, eating away at a section of this body and, if not treated, it will prevent the body entering into the kingdom of God, the Eternal Beatitude. This illness is the erosion of the dignity of those in the middle classes as they become imprisoned in our material world. The freedom they need to live in right relationship with God is eroded and the void being filled in ways that will not help them to be truly free. The church needs to find new ways of addressing this illness while continuing to nurture the other parts of the body. If this illness is tackled with the church's social teaching anew it will strengthen the whole body, as there will be a new awareness of its interconnectedness. This will move all people towards greater dignity and deepen the desire for a better world.

The jewels of the church's social teaching will only ever be of value if they are taken out of the treasure chest and worn in the hearts of the people of God. If we believe in Jesus Christ as our Redeemer, as the God of Justice, as the true revelation of God's hope for creation, as the way to God, we will have to be and want to be creators of a just world for all.[67] The dignity and vocation of the human person must underpin all our actions and decisions. For each person is treasured by God and precious in God's eyes. We must reveal and uphold this truth. The lives of others depend on us living our human vocation to its fullest.

Bibliography

Charles, R., & Maclean, D., *The Social Teaching of Vatican II* (San Francisco: Ignatius Press, 1982).

Catechism of the Catholic Church (Dublin: Veritas, 1994).

Dillon, R.S., *Dignity, Character and Self Respect* (New York: Routledge, 1995).

Dorr, D., *Spirituality and Justice* (Dublin: Gill & Macmillan, 1984).

Dorr, D., *Option for the Poor* (Dublin: Gill & Macmillan, 1983).

Flannery, A., *Vatican Council II* (Dublin: Dominican Publications, 1975).

James, G., *The Search for Faith and Justice in the 20th Century* (New York: Paragon House Publishers, 1987).

Gremillion, T., *The Gospel of Peace and Justice* (New York: Orbis Books, 1976).

Haughey, J., *The Faith that does Justice* (New York: Paulist Press, 1977).

Kelly, K., *New Directions in Moral Theology* (London: Geoffrey Chapman, 1992).

Komonchak, T. A., Collins, M., Lane, D. A., ed. *The New Dictionary of Theology* (Minnesota: The Liturgical Press, 1987).

---

67. Gaffney outlines three ways in which our understanding of faith in God is necessary for creating a just society: 'first, as a kind of enlightenment, necessary for envisaging a just society, second, as a kind of empowerment, necessary for effecting a just society, and third, as a kind of qualification, necessary for comprising a just society', op. cit. p 131.

Neuner, T., & Depuis, J., *The Christian Faith in the Doctrinal Documents of the Catholic Church* (New York: Alba House, 2001).

McDonagh, C., 'Redemptor Hominis' in *The Furrow* (Maynooth: The Furrow Trust, 1979), vol. 30 October.

Mahoney, T., *The Redemption and Human Dignity* (England: Catholic Truth Society, year not listed)

Leo XIII, *Rerum Novarum* 1891 (http://www.vatican.va/holy-father/leo-xiii/encyclicals/documents/hf-/-xiii-enc-15.51891-rerum-novarum-en.html.)

Paul VI, *Populorum Progressio* (London: Catholic Truth Society, 1967).

Synod of Bishops, Justice in the World 1971 (Athlone: St. Paul Publications, 1971).

Paul VI, *Evangelii Nuntiandi* (London Catholic Truth Society,1975).

John Paul II, *Redemptor Hominis* (London: Catholic Truth Society, 1979).

John Paul II, *Sollicitudo Rei Socialis* (Dublin: Veritas, 1987).

CHAPTER NINE

Subsidiarity, UN-habitat and Parish Work in Kenya

Gerard Whelan SJ

I am pleased to be asked to write this article as an Irish Jesuit. I don't often get requests that have anything to do with being Irish. I have not actually lived in Ireland since 1986. In that year I left to work in Zambia as part of my formation before ordination. I now find myself a 45 year-old parish priest in a slum parish in Nairobi. I am a member of the Eastern African Province of the Jesuits. I teach pastoral theology in the Jesuit School of Theology in this city and have a number of other commitments outside parish work, one of which, in particular, I wish to talk about here.

The parish where I work is located near to the Apostolic Nunciature in Nairobi. Four years ago I was asked to start helping to represent the Holy See to some United Nations agencies that have headquarters in Nairobi. The Catholic Church, under the legal title of The Holy See, has the privilege of being considered an observer nation at the highest levels of the United Nations. Most UN agencies are centred either in New York or in Geneva. However, the agencies for environment (UNEP) and for shelter (UN-Habitat) are headquartered in a major complex of United Nations offices in Nairobi. I mostly attend meetings of UN-Habitat. Let me explain some of the details of this work in UN-Habitat, how I understand the term subsidiarity, and how I have been part of some successful efforts within the agency to assist member nations commit themselves to employ this principle in formulating policy.

The Work of UN-Habitat

Like many United Nations agencies UN-Habitat is essentially

aimed at assisting governments to agree on development goals and to achieve them. The goals involved with UN-Habitat are those of assisting the populations of all countries attain adequate shelter. The work of UN-Habitat does include a concern for rural dwellers but, in practice, its primary energy becomes devoted to questions of how to conduct slum renewal in developing countries.

There is a growing awareness of the problem of slums by governments around the world. Today the population of the world is estimated to be 6.1 billion. Of these one billion are believed to live in extreme poverty. Of this one billion, 750 million are believed to live in cities, that is, in slums. The number of urban poor is expected to increase dramatically as the proportion of the world's overall population living in cities increases. In 1800, 2% of the world's population lived in cities, in 1950 the proportion was 30%. Today the proportion is 50% and in 2030 it is expected to be 60%. A conclusion that UN-Habitat is eager to impress on governments is that worldwide poverty is urbanising.

How then, should governments try to alleviate urban poverty and improve the conditions of slum dwellers? Obviously this is an enormous challenge and not one where any one UN-agency will have all the answers. For example, general questions of economic growth in a country are relevant here. If a country can achieve significant growth rates (hopefully in a way that is environmentally sustainable) and find ways to maximise the participation of poor people in this growth, this will be of the greatest significance for addressing problems of urban poverty. It is worth noting in passing that China, home to a quarter of the world's population, has succeeded in eliminating slums.

UN-Habitat officials link up with officials of many other UN agencies in the process of advising governments on issues of shelter. Then, they also identify a variety of specific issues on which they have something particular to contribute. One example would be investigating the complex questions of helping slum-dwellers obtain a plot of land with secure tenure and then making loans for house-building available for them. Another issue can be simply making sure that water supplies and sanitation services are available to the urban poor.

PART ONE

Subsidiarity and Decentralised Government
Another important issue with which UN-Habitat concerns itself is the importance of decentralisation of government structures. This needs a little explaining and is the place where the principle of subsidiarity becomes invoked. The point here is that no two slums are ever exactly the same. What is needed in upgrading will always vary. Consequently, governments should never think there can be a universal model for slum upgrading. What is needed is good local government that can enter into dialogue with local grass-root community groups and make decisions about upgrading. Before speaking more about the question of dialogue with community groups, let me speak more about the principle of subsidiarity and how it can be applied to this question.

Origins and Use of the Principle of Subsidiarity
The first use of the term subsidiarity in political philosophy was in Germany in the early modern era. At this time a process began whereby relatively independent city-states were persuaded to join a unified German Empire. The political representatives of these city-states negotiated certain rights for their cities as they allied themselves with the Empire. They jealously guarded these rights and the term subsidiarity was coined to express these rights. Basically, the cities only permitted authority to the imperial government over issues that could not be dealt with by local city governments. Examples of appropriate imperial government responsibilities included defence, foreign policy, and empire-wide economic policy formation. Examples of local responsibilities included road building, local water and sanitation provision, education and local economic decision-making. The city reserved the right to impose its own taxation on citizens in

addition to taxation levied on the same individuals for support of the imperial administration.

A next step in the history of wider awareness of this principle of governance was its co-option into the social encyclical of Pope Pius XI *Quadragessimo anno* published in 1932. It was a German Jesuit philosopher who contributed this idea to the Pope's thought. At the time, the church was particularly worried about expansive communism and the way the all-powerful state was interfering in the lives of families and individuals, not least in matters of religion. Let me offer a definition of how the term has come to be understood in this and other encyclicals:

> Subsidiarity is a principle in governance whereby a community of a higher order should not interfere in the internal life of a community of a lower order, depriving the latter of its functions, but rather should support it in case of need, and help to coordinate its activity with the activities of the rest of society, always with a view to the common good. (*Catechism of the Catholic Church,* par 1883.)

Quadragessimo anno had considerable influence. One example of this was that the principle of subsidiarity was discussed on the floor at the United Nations in 1948 when the Universal Declaration of Human Rights was being formulated. The term did not actually find its way into the declaration, but a proposal influenced by it did appear. In Paragraph 26C of the Declaration parents are declared to have a 'prior right' over the state in making decisions about the education of their children.

A next step in this story brings us to Marseilles, France. In the 1930s a young mayor in that city decided that his council needed to build a local primary school. To his dismay, he found that this was delayed for years because he needed to enter into elaborate negotiations with no less than five national government ministries in Paris so as to obtain permission for this. The mayor was scandalised by this experience. He found intellectual support for his complaint in *Quadragessimo anno* and the principle of subsidiarity enunciated there. He devoted the remainder of his long life to promoting the principle of subsidiarity in French law. He won considerable success, especially with regard to urban governance. At this same time, the early steps of what would become the European Union were being taken. Our mayor succeeded in influencing the social-political philosophy of the nascent European Union. Today, the European Union has adopted a 'European Charter of Local Government' that is based on the principle of subsidiarity. Various other policies of this organisation are based on the same principle. The manner in which Ireland benefited for so long from European regional development funds is related to the manner in which the principle of subsidiarity guides the philosophy of the European Union.

Subsidiarity and UN-Habitat
Returning to the affairs of UN-Habitat, the delegation of the Holy See has been happy to promote the acceptance of the vocabulary of subsidiarity in official statements of this agency as a way of promoting the kind of decentralised governance that can assist slum dwellers. It has not always been easy to persuade national governments to be open to this question. After all, decentralisation requires of national politicians that they limit some of their own powers and delegate them to others. A particular concern of the governments of many developing countries is that they already enjoy only a fragile national unity. Such governments express a concern that decentralisation could result in national fragmentation. Another issue is that the term subsidiarity is an unfamiliar one to citizens of Asia and the Americas and so the value of employing it to promote decentralisation is not always clear.

At any rate, this topic was much discussed in the bi-annual Governing Council of UN-Habitat for 2003. Participating in this event was exciting for me. No doubt readers have seen photographs of the general assembly hall of the United Nations in New York. Well, Nairobi boasts a hall that is somewhat similar. Representatives from each nation sit at a desk bearing the name of their country. I find myself behind the sign for 'Holy See'. Nearby are Germany, Hungary, Israel etc.

At the 2003 governing council, our delegation took a prominent role in proposing that, in spite of the fears of certain members, decentralisation is a valuable goal in national political arrangements. We further proposed that appealing to a principle of subsidiarity is a helpful way to promote this. My role at these meetings is basically only advisory. It is either the Papal Nuncio or his secretary who make the main speeches. However, meetings occur in different halls and I do find myself making speeches at times. One moving moment for me was trying to explain the notion of subsidiarity to the floor. I faced many mystified but curious faces as I made my effort. I took the term from the 26C of the Universal Declaration of Human Rights and spoke about subsidiarity in terms of 'prior right'. I spoke of how subsidiarity brings a deeper living of democracy because people tend to feel more involved in local groups than in wider national debates. When the small groups they are part of are acknowledged to have certain 'prior rights' to make decisions over and above higher levels of government, people can feel truly empowered. While speaking, I remembered Pope John Paul II speaking of how the Catholic Church claims to be 'expert on humanity'. I felt this as I spoke. We were not explicitly proclaiming Catholic faith, but we were presuming to teach representatives of national governments how best to live out democracy.

And what is more, they listened! The principle of subsidiarity was explicitly incorporated into the final document of the Governing Council. Now that governments have accepted to do this, they accept to be challenged by UN-Habitat and by other advocates regarding how much they have adopted subsidiarity in formulating policies concerning shelter in their countries. Another moving moment occurred at the final plenary session after this vote was taken. A member of the delegation from Russia came over in tears and spoke to the secretary of the Nuncio, an Irishman, Fr Michael Crotty from Fermoy. The Russian thanked Fr Crotty for his contribution. He spoke of how both his region and he personally had suffered under the centralised Moscow government in Soviet times.

PART 2

Subsidiarity in a Wider Sense
To date within UN-Habitat the term subsidiarity is used for supporting the empowering of local government with respect to central government. Our delegation of the Holy See still has our work cut out to encourage the use of the term for smaller scale community organisations – down as far as the family. To explain this point, I need to begin a somewhat roundabout explanation.

What is Community in a Slum?
There is a kind of mantra of best practice at UN-Habitat meetings that a key reason for empowering local governments in the area of slum renewal is so that they can enter into dialogue with local community groups in slums and negotiate agreed manners of renewing the slum. If, for example, many structures are too near to a railway line, local government needs to offer resettlement for the people whose structures will be demolished under a new plan for better order in the slum. Other parts of the slum may remain but receive better services. We cannot be naïve and think that every slum dweller can be persuaded to agree with the plan, but a substantial degree of agreement can be obtained when negotiation is well conducted. There are success stories from cities like Mumbai (Bombay), India in this matter. Soweto in South Africa has received so much renewal attention that it is no longer considered a slum. However, in many places, not least Nairobi, this negotiating process can be fraught with difficulties. One commentator at a meeting stated: 'we need to be very careful about making assumptions about knowing what community is in a slum or who represents it'.

Slums can be places of great division. In Nairobi slums, lines of division occur first between landlords and tenants. Secondly, ethnic divisions are strong, with different 'villages' within the slums housing people from different ethnic groups. Thirdly, and perhaps most fundamental of all, family life is very broken down in many slums. So single mothers live separately from men who live in groups in their own houses. Evidence is clear that domestic violence against both women and children increases when men are not 'tied in' to direct family responsibility.

The Faith-based Organisation and the Slums
A conclusion from the above reflections is that when you start speaking about community in slums you have to start thinking normatively as much as empirically. Community is often more an ideal to be worked towards than an already existing reality. Let me offer a working definition of community: It is a grouping of people who have similar experience, similar understanding and judgement of what it is that they have experienced, and similar decisions about how they need to act together. At UN-Habitat, the Holy See tends to make two points about this normative approach to community building in slums. The first is that attention needs to be paid to supporting family life where there is a man acting as responsible husband and father. The second is that governments should be aware that it is often religious organisations that are doing the best work in combating the social disintegration that occurs in slums, and building real community.

There is a term that is making an appearance in academic discussions of development: 'The Faith Based Organisation,' or 'FBO'. This term is placed along side that of the Non Governmental Organisation as one constituent of civil society. At UN-Habitat the Holy See often promotes the use of this term. In this context, I myself often speak of the work we do in my parish concerning the formation of 'Small Christian Communities'. These neighbourhood-sized groups are the foundation of parish life. Lay people meet there once a week. They pray with the Bible and try to relate the readings to their daily lives. They then also conduct various acts of service in their neighbourhood: these include ministry to the poor, ministry to the sick, ministry of justice and peace, ministry of family counselling. I speak with enthusiasm on this matter because I really believe that this is where we build the 'New Kenya'. There is a culture of selfishness, division, and corruption that has prevailed at government level in Kenya for many years. Inevitably this influences how people relate to each other even at neighbourhood level in slums. By being members of Small Christian Communities, Catholics begin to form a 'counter-culture' within their neighbourhood and to have a real effect on others.

Back to Subsidiarity
Let me now wheel my argument back to subsidiarity. At UN-Habitat there has been clear agreement about employing the terminology of subsidiarity just as far, so to speak, as empowered local government. A task of the Holy See, first of all, is to point out that, logically, this term should also apply to the manner in which local government should let local community groups and even families make the kind of decisions that are appropriate to them. This is especially relevant in the context of slum upgrading where local government needs to find such interlocutors so as to agree on changes that need to be made. A subsequent insight is that often such community groups hardly exist in slums. Instead of finding local voices that express the common good, one finds sectional interests promoting their own agenda. These voices can represent only the landlords, or only one ethnic group, or sometimes, let me admit, only one religion or denomination. If local government is serious about wanting to find real community groups with which to dialogue they must switch to thinking normatively. The must think about how they can help build such community. I have heard one theorist speak about how important it can be to build sports facilities in poor areas if you want to build community. However, another key point promoted by the Holy See at Habitat is that local government should think of new ways of supporting Faith Based Organisations as they perform their tasks of community building based on religious motivation. One way and another, the principle of subsidiarity can be invoked as a reason for doing this.

Conclusion
In this article I have written about how I have collaborated in

employing Catholic social teaching in one area where I minister – UN-Habitat. I have had the exiting experience of how the ideas of the Catholic Church can be well received at a multi-lateral level. In a number of ways, delegates from other governments find that Catholic social teaching is a kind of 'best kept secret'. We tend to communicate ideas that are just not attended to by the kind of academic and civil servant advisers that governments otherwise listen to. When promoting the use of the principle of subsidiarity we were promoting a notion that is strictly philosophical – we were not presuming that listeners needed to be people of religious faith in order to appreciate our point. However, when speaking to other national delegates I felt proud to be Catholic. I really did feel how it is from our position of faith in Jesus Christ that we are able to switch to a more secular set of ideas and still speak to others as 'experts in humanity'.

CHAPTER TEN

Catholic Social Teaching in Education

David Tuohy SJ

Catholic social teaching seems to promote two dimensions – the world of thought and the world of action. The world of thought introduces us to ideas, values and principles that can guide our choices in public and private. The world of action demands that these principles be translated practically into our lives. Familiarity with the world of thought is not enough. Clear thinking leads to a demand to put the theory into practice. It is the old idea that faith, without good works, is dead. Schools are ideal places for young people (and indeed teachers and parents) to develop both dimensions – by exploring the key principles for social action, and by engaging in acts of solidarity with others as a way of seeing these principles in action. This chapter looks at four different influences of social teaching in education – the changing Irish context; an extended reflection on the world of thought as applied to a philosophy of education, and shorter reflections on the issues in the governance of education and on developing social action programmes in schools.

Context

To say that Catholic education in Ireland is going through a period of major change is an understatement. The context in which Catholic education takes place is very different from the context of 20 years ago. The value system of society is now regarded as secular, almost post-Christian. There is a sense of disillusion with institutions in general, and with the church in particular. The power position once held by the church is rejected and there is a suspicion of many of its pronouncements in the light of previous abuses. Also, the role of education, and particularly educational credentials, has changed radically. We now have mass participation in second-level education, and it is a pathway to third level education for over 50% of any student cohort. Third level qualifications are almost essential in order to access high paying jobs. To a certain extent, these qualifications are the new indicators of wealth, replacing land and class. The pressure to access third level courses has impacted on the culture of second level schools, as achievement in second level is used as a means of selection to third level. This has given rise to a more utilitarian view of second level education as young people strive to find a position in the so-called 'meritocratic' selection system. There is also greater emphasis on life-long learning, both in the development of post-graduate qualifications at third level and as second chance education for those who missed out on earlier chances. This changing context affects religious, teachers, parents and students alike.

This cultural change is matched by structural changes within schools. The governance profile in schools has changed considerably in recent years. We see a growth in the number of community schools and a changing role for VEC schools. Within the voluntary secondary schools under Catholic management, there is a major decline of religious personnel and a growth of lay people in leadership roles and in teaching religious education. Religious congregations are looking to the future of trusteeship, and a time when they will no longer be available to manage the schools. In this context, there is an increased demand for Catholic schools to develop a vibrant sense of mission and vision that responds to both the tradition in which they were founded, and also proclaims an attractive philosophy of education for today's world.

I work with religious congregations and with schools in developing a perspective on Catholic education, both at a strategic level and in developing policies that reflect these values in practice. Together, we reflect on core gospel values and on church documents about education and schooling. In general, our reflection begins with the Vatican Council, and the key documents

EDUCATION

that place a context on the work of education – *Lumen Gentium* (The Church), *Gaudium et Spes* (The Church in the Modern World), *Dei Verbum* (Divine Revelation) and *Gravissimum Educationis* (Declaration on Christian Education). Since 1965, there have been four major documents on education – *The Catholic School* (1977), *Lay Catholics in Schools: Witness to Faith* (1982), *The Religious Dimension of Education in a Catholic School* (1988), *The Catholic School on the Threshold of the Third Millennium* (1998), as well as the documents on social teaching that inform a general approach to work and social organisation. A key function of our reflection is to articulate a vision of Catholic education that is in line with social teaching and makes a valuable contribution to Irish society. A second function is to support the process of faith formation in schools. Here the social teaching is a core element of the syllabus that students reflect on as part of the school programme.

Philosophy of Education

> The school is a centre in which a specific concept of the world, of the person and of history is developed and conveyed.
> (*The Catholic School*, par 8).

The inspiring aspect of church documents is the positive view of the human person. This belies the somewhat turgid (and politically incorrect with regard to gender) prose which introduced the Vatican II document on education:

> In fulfilling the mandate she has received from her divine Founder to proclaim the mystery of salvation to all men, and to restore all things in Christ, Holy Mother the church must be concerned with the whole of man's life, even the earthly part of it insofar as that has a bearing on his heavenly calling.
> (*GE*, introduction)

Four main themes arise from the documents that clarify the Christian philosophy of the person:
- Human beings are made in God's image and from this is derived the dignity of each person

- The divine spark exists within each of us, and we are called to allow this grace to develop within us
- We are both blessed and broken, and we experience this tension in our relations with others and in our successes and failures
- We have a future and destiny beyond this world, and this gives us hope in the face of adversity

This philosophy gives rise to a holistic view of human development, especially the development of young people. It places a major challenge of how we relate to one another in schools, as well as the approach we take to the content we teach. The documents show great sensitivity to dealing with young people in a way that is appropriate to their age. *The Catholic School* (1977) focuses on experiential learning that is meaning-centred, urging teachers to 'help spell out the meaning of (students') experiences and their truths'. It specifically warns that 'any school which neglects this duty and which offers merely pre-cast conclusions' hinders the personal development of its pupils (par 27).

The perspective on human history is filled with a sense of the activity of the Holy Spirit, constantly forging a new creation, and bringing it to perfection. This involves learning from our experiences, and also a call to further work.

- God reaches out to us in our day-to-day lives, and is active in history through the Holy Spirit
- Christians have a history and are called to shape history, to help the coming of the kingdom

Both of these themes are very much in line with the worldview of St Ignatius in the *Spiritual Exercises*. For me, this view of the world of study is refreshingly open. It goes beyond a narrow view of a disembodied spiritual existence, which is focused almost entirely on devotional practices. It transcends the former suspicion of culture, and particularly the world of science as being opposed to religion. This attitude is outlined in the opening paragraph of Vatican II's document on Christian Education:

EDUCATION

> Enjoying more leisure, as they sometimes do, men *(sic!)* find that remarkable developments in technology and in scientific investigation, and new means of social communication offer them readier opportunities for attaining their inheritance of intellectual and spiritual culture, and for fulfilling themselves and one another by forging stronger bonds between various groups and even whole people. (*GE*, introduction)

Reflecting on the social context in which education takes place, the church documents place a strong emphasis on the role of the family, and also on the role of the school in promoting social change, both in the way it prepares its students and in its own service to the poor and marginalised.

- Family and society are the natural contexts for human life – in them we find our identity
- Society, its structures and its institutions can and should be improved
- Christians are called to share Jesus' identification with the poor

These statements have implications for the development of partnership between schools and parents, for policies on admission to Catholic schools and for curriculum development. I would like to conclude this section by looking at the implications for curriculum development, and take up the other points in the next section.

In 1972, the American Bishops published a reflection on Vatican II's *Declaration on Christian Education*. It was entitled *To Teach as Jesus Did*, in which they summarised the purpose of Catholic Education as:

- The delivery of Jesus' *message*
- The formation of Christian *Community*
- The witness of *service* in Jesus' name
- The centrality of *worship* (added in a 1990 review of the document)

This document gives a holistic view of the culture of the Catholic school, as it focuses on Catholic identity in the US, where the church is a (sizeable) minority group. It is an impressive and challenging document, although it tends to work from a 'closed' view of Catholic identity. The document does not address in detail the contribution of different areas of the curriculum to student development. This contrasts with the curriculum outline of the Catholic Education Office, Sydney. Its document *The Curriculum in the Catholic School* (1991), sees curriculum as a means:

- To assist in the total development of the individual student; religious, intellectual, aesthetic, social, emotional, physical
- To educate students in their Catholic faith and to invite them to commit themselves to a life centred on Jesus and his values
- To develop each student's ability to engage in clear thinking, discerning judgement and responsible decision-making
- To promote a deep sense of appreciation of and responsibility for the natural environment
- To foster the critical assimilation of culture
- To cultivate the skills necessary for finding personal meaning and leading a productive life as a member of a community
- To develop a particular awareness in students of being called to be positive agents of change in society
- To promote a commitment to justice, peace and the development of self and others
- To enhance each student's capacity to think and experience creatively and intuitively

In summary:
- To assist in the integration of faith, culture and life experience

These points are a good summary of the key issues raised in church documents. In Ireland, there is not much dispute that these are reasonable goals for the curriculum. The key issue for schools is to see how this operates. To a large extent, the process is facilitated by the general statement of the purpose of education in the Education Act, and also the thrust of developments from the National Council for Curriculum and Assessment (NCCA). In particular, in their discussion document on developing Social, Personal and Health Education at senior cycle (2003), they give an expanded view of the holistic nature of student development, including areas such as: aesthetic, creative, cultural, emotional, intellectual, moral, physical, political, religious, social and spiritual. There is strong emphasis on discovery learning in the Junior Cycle, Transition Year and the Leaving Certificate Applied. These developments find an easy home in the social teaching of the church.

Perhaps one area that does not sit so well in Irish society at the moment is the second statement from the Sydney document – to educate students in their Catholic faith and to invite them to commit themselves to a life centred on Jesus and his values. There seems to be a reluctance to identify strongly with the church dimension of the school, opting instead for the more generic Christian or gospel values. Part of this is a recognition of a more pluralist Irish society, where many of the students are not 'churched', and there is a growing non-Catholic and even non-Christian student base. This has particular implications for Catholic schools as the main providers of education, and in receipt of government funds for an education policy that is committed more to the common good than it is to promoting denominational education.

In the *New Catechism*, the main section on education is under Marriage and the Family. Here, it is stated that 'education is service'. This service is seen as preparing children to love, to be mature adults, and to be independent. It is in this section that we get a glimpse of the hope that education will bring for human development. A similar theme is to be found in the section 'The Business of Living'. In these paragraphs, we read the following description:

> People live with an eye on the clock, waiting for the weekend, counting the days to their holidays. They work to live. A very real and human life is lived in the times when we are 'free'. (437-8)

This separation of work and living is often detrimental to the quality of life, a theme that is consistent in social teaching. This separation can begin in school, if learning is seen as a burden geared to performance in examinations. In a piece of research from the 1950s, Coleman described schools as places where youth culture took place. He found the activity of school to be something that most young people tolerated because it gave them opportunities to be with their peers and to have a 'real life' during breaks. It would seem to be a pity that learning could not be seen as fun, for both the pupil and the teacher. Creating the learning school is a key role for School Development Planning, and it is hoped that the experience of learning will give rise to a commitment to life-long learning, and a sense of living life to the full. The social teaching of the church promotes a very positive and holistic view of the human person, and of the role of school in promoting human development. It is exciting to be involved in exploring its implications, and helping people name what they are doing as part of their mission as Christian educators.

Governance

In the past, the church was mainly involved in an education *for Catholics*. There was a strong internal emphasis on an institutional model of church. This shows itself in church documents in a strong (and at times strident) emphasis on the right of the church to establish schools, and the duty of parents to send their children to Catholic schools, where possible. This reflected the historical reality of the church in many countries. For instance, in Ireland, the Catholic education system was born out of the struggle to establish a strong Catholic Church in a society where it had no voice. There was a mix of nationalism and piety, and the aim of church involvement in education was to promote a strong social mobility in order to allow Catholics take their place in society and influence its politics. The approach was largely successful, and it was this mindset in education that was exported by Irish missionaries to many places. To a large extent, the driving vision was to develop the church triumphant, and to establish the church as a serious political institution. Certainly, in my own religious education in secondary school, I was more informed about apologetics than I was about scripture.

One impact of Vatican II was that the church began to speak of herself in new ways. Dulles described these in terms of models, each of which emphasised a different aspect of a rich tradition. The post-Vatican II era was characterised by a rejection of the institutional certainties of the past and by self-doubt when teaching catechetics, where apologetics gave way to free discussion on moral issues. In religious congregations, there was a major call to rediscover the charism of the Founders. This shift was a movement away from the *church* as the driving vision, to discovering the fundamental vision of the *gospel message* at the core of all congregations. There was a major emphasis on the community dimension of the church, at both a liturgical and an apostolic level. In education, there has been a movement to reflect on 'Catholic Education for All'. This approach looks to develop a theology and spirituality *of* education and schooling, rather than a focus on theology and spirituality *in* education. In the previous section, we saw some of the implications of this for curriculum issues in the Catholic school. There are three other areas that impact on this development: the changing student body, partnerships and leadership roles.

Changing student body
The churches have been the main providers of secondary education in Ireland. As a result of this contribution, the state now enjoys a healthy infrastructure for the provision of education, and the church is in a privileged position in terms of attracting students. I have outlined above how the demographic context of the school-going population has changed. This challenges the schools to define the Catholic character of the school, being faithful to its traditional mission and at the same time being of service to national education policies. The most recent document from the Vatican on education, *The Catholic School on the Threshold of the Third Millennium*, called for the renewal of Catholic schools in the light of many changes in the field of education, especially the development of lifelong learning. It sets the work of Catholic education clearly in the field of evangelisation.

> It is not merely a question of adaptation, but of missionary thrust, the fundamental duty to evangelise, to go towards men and women wherever they are, so that they may receive the gift of salvation. (par 3)

In the course of the document (pars 5-7) it outlines many of the challenges facing schools, including issues of secularisation, religious indifference and non-practice. By placing the schools firmly in the model of the evangelising church, this document challenges many of the practices of Irish schools, which are more used to models of supporting students whose families were deeply rooted in the tradition and symbolism of the Christian story and the Catholic church.

There is another aspect of the changing student body that reflects a growing pluralism in Irish society, with people from different cultures looking for education. The question for Catholic schools is how to integrate different traditions while maintaining a Catholic character. Part of the solution is in the schools' self-understanding as the People of God, where the presence of cultural differences offers the opportunity for inter-cultural dialogue and learning. This is a new reality for Irish schools, and it is a challenge that is being faced by a largely lay teaching force. In this area, the social teaching of the church offers more encouragement than definite guidelines.

Partnerships
Both the rhetoric of Catholic social teaching and Irish government policy describe a partnership approach to education. In Catholic social teaching the partners are the home, the school and the parish. In Ireland, partnerships with parents exist at a formal level. Nationally, parents are represented with other partners on policy committees, and at school level, there is formal representation on the Board of Management. In the area of faith formation, schools have been slow to engage with parents. Those schools that have been successful have found core groups of parents who are themselves hungry for spiritual nourishment, and who find an application of the approaches offered to the children very beneficial to their own needs.

EDUCATION

The fact that so many of the second-level schools in Ireland have been run by religious congregations has often meant a lack of immediate involvement with the local parish. In some cases there have been local difficulties identifying parish responsibility, especially with a large catchment area. As a result, schools have often developed a mini-parish, which has nourished the faith of young people, but has failed to provide links so that the nourishment might be continued when they leave school. Now when schools try to make links, they find that parish clergy are also an ageing group and spread thinly on the ground. Indeed, in some parishes, there has also been a lack of partnership with lay people in developing a vibrant faith community.

> It is also helpful to bear in mind, in harmony with the Second Vatican Council, that this community dimension in the Catholic school is not a merely sociological category; it has a theological foundation as well. The educating community, taken as a whole, is thus called to further the objective of a school as a place of complete formation through interpersonal relations. (*Third Millennium,* par 18)

The challenge here is to take the social teaching on partnership seriously. This means offering both opportunities and supports to different groups to have a strong voice in the development of 'that personalised approach which is needed for an educational project to be efficacious'. (par 20)

Leadership Roles
A third area for governance is in the development of leadership roles. This has a focus in two areas – in trusteeship and in the support and training of leaders. With the decline in numbers of religious, new possibilities for trusteeship are developing. Religious Congregations, both individually and collaboratively, are searching for new structures of Trustee Boards, many of which will involve lay trustees. There has been a lot of activity in developing 'ethos' statements that will be the core responsibility of these Boards. This has exciting challenges, but also has a num-

ber of pitfalls. There is a strong danger that Trustee Boards will be given an impossible task – to preserve an ethos that was developed in different times, to meet different challenges. What is needed is the same trust in the Holy Spirit working in these groups, and a similar creativity and flexibility in responding to the challenges of evangelisation that perhaps the founding congregations never had to face. There is a danger that Religious Congregations, as they disengage from education, will leave demands on their lay successors that they themselves could not, and did not in the past, meet.

In general, the areas of Catholic social teaching applied to organisations are not directly applied to education. Yet, the themes of the common good, solidarity, subsidiarity, collaboration, co-responsibility, partnership and community are key values that permeate church documents on both social teaching and education. In Ireland, we are more familiar with these concepts from the rhetoric of recent government legislation on education through the Education Act, than we are from the experience of working in Catholic schools. Yet, the ideal is there. In the media, we have plenty of evidence of the church at its worst – focused on power and on dominance. In the social teachings, we have the church at its best – fully committed to the poor and the marginalised, as well as empowering individuals in their own worlds. A challenge for future structures is to avoid an overly centralised, hierarchical and paternalistic approach and to model the type of organisation that is promoted in its own social teaching.

Currently, Catholic schools in Ireland are being very well served by the first generation of lay principals. Many of these principals have taught side-by-side with religious colleagues. They have imbibed the value system through observation, imitation and dialogue. However, we are now preparing for a second generation of lay leaders, who will have had minimum contact with religious teachers. There is a need to develop a greater level of theological literacy and eloquence, and to develop an appropriate spirituality of service that combines the world of work, of family and of church mission. The challenge here is to affirm the central role of lay people in the mission of the church, and to transcend the traditional paternalism that saw them as excellent helpers to a predominantly clerical church.

Social Action
In the previous sections I have looked at the impact the church's social teaching *on* education has on my work – as inspiration and direction. However, the church's social teaching must also play a key role *in* education. This is linked with the world of action, which is made up of two elements. The first of these is the immediate experience of working directly with those in need. Here the focus is on the individual in need of support. The response is immediate and short term. A second element is when one works on policies and structures in society to bring about a more long-term justice. This element requires a different kind of commitment, a commitment that is likely to be sustained only through a more explicit understanding of why one commits oneself to this work.

In many schools, we find young people actively engaged in social outreach programmes. In particular, many Transition Year and Leaving Certificate Applied students have social outreach as a core element of their programmes. The students work with older members of the community, with children suffering from mental or physical disabilities, or they get involved in activities that alleviate poverty. In practice, many young people respond with great generosity in these outreach programmes and have a very positive influence on those they meet. They pick up the message that they are supposed to help people in need. Yet, they often have very little idea as to why they do it. They can not talk with any eloquence about key ideas of the common good, a preferential option for the poor, respect for the life and dignity of the human person, or solidarity. These are the key ideas that explain why we become involved in social activities. These ideas help us reflect on our experience of activity at a deeper level. It affirms that experience as part of our Christian commitment and helps us deepen that commitment.

Perhaps the weakest element of our education system is the way we help young people reflect on their experiences. Sometimes, the structures we give them to develop their critical analysis of society and culture are very surface. It is here that exposure to the social teaching of the church can provide young people with the necessary tools for that reflection. In the new Junior Certificate Religion programme, young people are introduced to morality as personal decision-making. In the new Leaving Certificate Religion programme, the syllabus has an optional module on Justice and Peace that aims:
- To introduce the principles and skills of social analysis
- To encourage the application of these principles and skills in the local context, and in a selection of national and global contexts
- To identify and analyse the links between religious belief and commitment and action for justice and peace
- To explore the relationship between the concepts of justice and peace and the challenge to sustain this relationship, particularly in relation to the Irish context

(NCCA syllabus outline – section F)

This syllabus gives the teacher ample opportunity to introduce the social teaching of the church in understanding different concepts of justice and peace, and in tracing the development of Christian thought on this subject. In designing the course, it was hoped that students 'should be afforded an opportunity to engage in extended reflection, research and analysis', and that the results of this process be submitted for assessment. Whether individual schools opt to include Religion as an exam subject or not, the challenge remains for them to help young people reflect on these issues as part of their formation and spiritual sensibility.

Conclusion

In this chapter I have tried to outline some of the key developments in Catholic education in Ireland, and how the social teaching of the church impacts on a vision for the future, as well as how it can become a core element of the faith formation programme. This is an exciting time in Irish education as we move from an intuitive to an articulated understanding of the mission of Catholic education. It is my strong belief that Catholic schools can offer an attractive, value-laden formation that many parents will want for their children. The shift in pedagogy from a suspicion of indoctrination to a facilitation of critical thought is evidence of a growing awareness of the key principles of social teaching in the Catholic school. The current challenges focus around the creation of new structures to empower and support schools run by lay people, and to find creative ways of helping young people engage with the commitment of a life of faith committed to justice.

CHAPTER ELEVEN

Solidarity in Catholic Social Teaching

Cathy Molloy

Probably at no time in the history of humanity has the notion of solidarity and its exercise been more keenly and intuitively understood and acted on than in the days and weeks following the disaster caused by the tidal wave in South East Asia in December 2004. Due to the power of modern media technology, the shock and horror of the disaster unfolded in the homes of people around the world within hours of its occurrence. And, as the tragedies of its aftermath unfolded for the people immediately involved, there was an outpouring of shared emotion around the world – shock, horror, grief, fear, incomprehension, sympathy, anger, followed rapidly by the need and desire to *do* something. Individuals and groups, institutions, churches and governments reacted with what can be seen to be a truly human response to the plight of the suffering people. Solidarity took over and showed us that people really do care about their fellow human beings. Despite the inequities in many of the structures and systems we are all part of, we learn at first hand that it is more human to empathise with people in their suffering, it is more human to want to alleviate the pain of others, it is more human to do something practical – to go there, to be with the people, to give money or goods or time. It is more human to pray in solidarity with stricken humanity as we saw in the moving ceremony from Thailand where representatives of many faiths and churches gathered to remember those who lost their lives in this most awful of 'natural disasters'.

The social teaching of the church has consistently called for solidarity between people and peoples. In recent times the call has become more urgent and more focused with Popes, from

John XXIII in the sixties to John Paul II in the present, stressing solidarity as the appropriate relationship for authentic human progress and development. For example, in his 1961 encyclical *Mater et Magistra*, John XXIII spoke of solidarity, which 'binds all people together as members of a common family, making it impossible for wealthy nations to look with indifference on the plight of other nations whose citizens do not enjoy even basic human rights.'(157) He refers to the growing interdependence of nations and the impossibility of preserving a lasting peace while glaring economic and social inequalities persist. Paul VI in his 1967 encyclical letter on the Development of Peoples, *Populorum Progressio*, noting that the 'social question' has become worldwide, wrote, 'there can be no progress towards the complete development of man without the simultaneous development of all humanity in the spirit of solidarity.' (Without going into the issue of language in current church documents, and the use of 'man' as generic, it goes without saying that solidarity specifically in relation to gender was not yet a pressing issue for many people.) Paul VI goes on to ask a series of questions of those who have more than they need.

> Is he prepared to support out of his own pocket works and undertakings organised in favour of the most destitute? Is he ready to pay higher taxes so that the public authorities can intensify their efforts in favour of development? Is he ready to pay a higher price for imported goods so that the producer may be more justly rewarded, or to leave his country, if necessary and if he is young, in order to assist in this development of the young nations?[1]

It is not just recent weeks in Ireland that illustrate that there is an increasing number of people taking these questions seriously. The fact that the issue of higher taxes for badly-needed development of public services at home, and of the delivery of promised aid to developing countries, is heatedly, if spasmodically, dis-

---

1. Encyclical letter of Pope Paul VI, On the Development of Peoples, *Populorum Progressio*, 1967, 47.

cussed in the media by politicians and others is testimony to our taking it seriously as a nation. The question of linking fair trading conditions to the issue of development and debt relief for poorer nations has been gathering momentum.[2]

But never has the need for solidarity been more acute. The tsunami disaster shocked us into immediate response, but the daily death toll from the HIV-AIDS tidal wave, and the millions of our fellow human beings living with AIDS, directly or indirectly, although not brought to our screens in the same way, cry out for something of the same concern and sympathy and real engagement with them in their ongoing crisis. Enda Mc Donagh, in 'The Catholic Church and HIV/AIDS', (*The Furrow*, October 2004), reminds us that each of us is part of the body of human kind and that 'the whole human race has HIV-AIDS'. He reminds us too that 'In Catholic social teaching justice is the key to recognising the status and dignity of each person within the community in what might be called individual justice, while pursuing the overall good and equity of the community through social justice.'

What does solidarity mean?

So is it obvious then what we mean by solidarity and that we are doing it well enough?

Reflecting in 1982 on the experience of solidarity from the particular context of El Salvador, Jon Sobrino, a Jesuit priest, philosopher and theologian, who has spent his life working in that country, describes the movement of solidarity towards the people and the church of El Salvador. In *Theology of Christian Solidarity* (1982), his intention was to define, in Christian terms, the meaning and roots of solidarity, and to show what the 'rediscovery of solidarity' means for the church and for faith. The situ-

---

2. The International Jesuit Network for Development held a conference, *Debt and Trade: Time to Make the Connections*, in Dublin in Sept 2004, bringing together speakers from developing countries, the World Bank, the International Monetary Fund, and Development Cooperation Ireland. Papers, edited by the Centre for Faith and Justice, are to be published by Veritas in 2005.

ation of many people in that country was one of life in inhuman conditions whose most 'elemental human rights are utterly violated, and who are repressed in all their just strivings for liberation'. It is in the following description that we can see the evolving of solidarity as it has come to be understood in contemporary Catholic social thought.

> Many individuals and institutions have made the church of El Salvador their 'neighbour' in the gospel meaning of that term: they have not taken a detour in order to avoid seeing the wounded victim on the road, but instead have come closer to examine the situation and to help. Cardinals, archbishops, bishops, priests and religious men and women of the Catholic Church, delegations from Protestant churches, and theologians both Catholic and Protestant have come to this country. Many professional politicians, journalists, jurists, members of human rights organisations and aid agencies, have also come and many of them in addition to their professional capacity have shown their specific concern as Christians. They have carried out their visit in a Christian way, engaging in dialogue with church personnel, taking part in meetings and liturgical celebrations with other Christians and, most of all, coming close to suffering Salvadorans in the countryside, in jails, and in refugee camps.[3]

Sobrino goes on to describe the solidarity of those who could not come to El Salvador but made the Salvadorans really their 'neighbour'. This was achieved by means of letters from grassroots Christian communities all over the world, statements from bishops and Episcopal Conferences denouncing the repression and the violation of human rights, the sending of aid and the organisation of solidarity committees in many countries for the sharing of information, fund-raising, pressuring governments, organising liturgies and solidarity demonstrations. There were still others who came from outside and remained forever at the side of the people as martyrs.

3. *Theology of Christian Solidarity*, Jon Sobrino, Juan Hernandez Pico, tr. Orbis Books 1985.

What is most striking about his account is that solidarity is about engaging with people at a deep level and is fundamentally different from the giving of material aid which is obviously good and necessary and, as he points out, a correct response to the ethical imperative. Sobrino goes on to say that if solidarity were no more than material aid it would be no more than a magnified kind of almsgiving where givers offer something they own without thereby feeling a 'deep-down personal commitment' or without feeling any need to continue this aid. In authentic solidarity the first effort to give aid commits a person at a deeper level than that of mere giving and becomes an ongoing process and not a contribution. In other words, the giver too is changed in a way that is radical and ongoing.

In El Salvador, following the initial giving of aid, the giving and receiving churches set up relationships. It was not a matter of a one-way flow of aid but of mutual giving and receiving. It is this point that is crucial for an understanding of what solidarity actually means.

A value of the exercise carried out by Jon Sobrino is in its being transferable to other situations. Whether we are talking about solidarity between individuals or groups, churches or nations, the key to authenticity is in relationship, in recognising the interdependence and mutual giving and receiving that is involved. This is very different from the kind of solidarity that is an alliance to promote particular interests. According to Sobrino's account, solidarity begins when some churches help another church in need because it has taken on solidarity with the poor and oppressed among its own people. The helping churches find that they not only give but also receive from the church they aid. What they receive is of a different and higher order and they usually describe it as new inspiration in faith, and help in discovering their identities in human, ecclesial, and Christian terms, and in relationship to God. Through mutual giving and receiving the churches establish relationships and discover that in principle it is essential that a local church be united to another church, and that in principle this mutual relationship embraces all levels of life, from material aid to faith in God.

Another positive element for me is that it shows the interconnectedness of small steps and how together they can make a big difference. This gives the lie to the notion that we can do nothing to change things, and to the despondence of so many people about the enormity of many problems and situations and their capacity to change anything. Rather, the smallest step taken by an individual in authentic solidarity is of the greatest significance.

Solidarity in the teaching of John Paul II

Almost certainly the reflection published in 1985 by Jon Sobrino was influential in the presentation of the teaching on solidarity by John Paul II in his 1987 encyclical *Solicitudo Rei Socialis*, (38) and repeated in the 1988 encyclical *Christifideles Laici*, (42). Speaking about the active and responsible participation of all in public life, and of how we are, all of us, the goal of public life as well as its leading participants, he writes the following:

> (solidarity) is not a feeling of vague compassion or shallow distress at the misfortune of so many people, both near and far. On the contrary, it is a firm and persevering determination to commit oneself to the common good, that is to say, to the good of all and of each individual because we are all really responsible for all.

Of course it is not necessary to go to El Salvador in the past to find instances of authentic solidarity. I think of the ongoing commitment and relationships of Irish groups involved in, for example, the Chernobyl disaster, or the plight of children in some Romanian orphanages, or the many who have shown an enduring solidarity with people and places they initially reached out to in crisis. The giving and receiving, the reciprocity involved, are evident, and solidarity of this sort gives meaning and identity to those involved just as in Sobrino's example. Further, it would seem likely that authentic solidarity in one context would preclude the opposite of solidarity in other areas. Racism, classism, sexism, clericalism, lack of due care for the earth and other 'isms' are precluded by authentic solidarity with the other who suffers in these contexts.

In 1991 the Jesuit Centre for Faith and Justice published a booklet entitled *Solidarity: The Missing Link in Irish Society*. Times were very different then and the vision of solidarity was offered in a context of high unemployment, of pre-peace process Northern Ireland and a relatively indifferent Ireland *vis à vis* 'the troubles', of a church often seeming to work only from the values of the better off in society. Noting the generosity of the Irish people in giving aid to developing countries, the authors point out that it is more difficult for us to respond to problems that exist at home. In a section on 'Solidarity and Civic Life' the authors write:

> We are hampered by a terrible individualism. This has many aspects. It is in line with the pervasive individualism of the international capitalist culture which shapes and deforms our way of thinking, valuing, and acting, and which puts a tremendous stress on the achievements of the individual no matter how this affects the rest of society.[4]

They go on to highlight the need for structural solidarity. This would mean that we rely not just on attitudes and behaviour but that solidarity should be built into legal, social and economic institutions which would truly reflect the values of solidarity emerging more randomly in the culture. Has this been progressing over the period of the past ten years, or is there an unacknowledged battle going on in Irish society between the solidarity that we might all say we desire and the individualism that seems to grow in us as we become more wealthy?

---

4. *Solidarity: The Missing Link in Irish Society*, Tim Hamilton, Brian Lennon, Gerry O'Hanlon, Frank Sammon, Jesuit Centre for Faith and Justice, 1991, 14.

Wealthy Ireland

The signs of the new wealth that has been Ireland's in the last few years are everywhere. You couldn't keep up with the numbers of cranes that keep appearing, heralding new hotels and apartment blocks, houses and offices, shopping centres, and giant retail outlets. And that's just new building. Look at the home improvement situation and you can see extensions, and attic conversions, modernisations and regenerations, landscaped gardens and patios, and the accompanying gadgets and equipment needed to enjoy them. The numbers of new cars and drivers tell their own story in the clogged streets of our cities, towns and villages. The new roads ensure that ever bigger trucks and containers can transport ever more goods to every corner of Ireland, and indeed some in the other direction. Winter suntans, up until recently sported by the few, are now commonplace as many Irish people avail of year-round breaks, many in their own holiday homes in warmer climates. Then there is the health and beauty industry encompassing everything from haircare to beauty treatments and cosmetic surgery, and the accompanying advertising leading us to believe that this is so normal and almost to wonder how we ever managed without it all. And this is not yet to consider shops and supermarkets, department stores and specialist health or food shops, and the vast amount of goods to be bought and sold – food, clothes, household goods, sports gear, music and videos, DVDs and the latest iPods. Fitness and Leisure Centres, theatres, cinemas and galleries, restaurants, pubs and clubs, offering many kinds of entertainment are all part of the wheels of the new wealth, with the sex industry accounting for a not inconsiderable proportion. Goods and choices abound. Are we at saturation point yet? How much is enough?

> Our species is unique in its propensity to trade. We also are unique in the infinity of our desires. Most people feel that more income and more wealth is better than less, and this seems to apply with particular force to those who already have most. (*After the Celtic Tiger*, Clinch, Convery, Walsh, 2002.)

Thanks to this work from these three UCD professors, some simple economic facts about the new Ireland are made accessible to the non-expert reader. Total direct income increased by 61% over the five-year period to 2000. State transfer payments, for example, child benefit, increased by 11% for the same period. The top 10% of households in income terms spent on average over twice the national average expenditure of all households. For the lowest 10% of households expenditure was less than a quarter of the average for all households. The Central Statistics Office Gender Report, *Women and Men in Ireland 2004*, shows that one in four Irish women now run the risk of poverty, with female lone parents and older women particularly at risk. A 2004 ESRI report (Callan *et al*) shows relative income poverty rates in Ireland are considerably higher than the European Union average (though not as high as the USA). This has not changed with the years of increased wealth. Where is solidarity, Christian or other, in all of this? You don't need to be an expert to work out that relatively the gap between the richest and poorest in our society is enormous. Leaving aside the devastating effects of the most recent natural disaster, you don't have to be an international aid worker to know that this gap is even more evident between rich and poor nations. Who decides that this is acceptable and on what grounds? What values or guidelines are at the basis of such decisions?

It has been argued that in Ireland we are really in a catch-up situation relative to the rest of the pre-2004 EU member states. It is good that most of us in Ireland are finding out what it is like to enjoy material well-being. The fact is we have not just caught up but overtaken, in terms of private, individual consumption. Yet, already, there is a sense of slight unease. There are mutterings here and there about the affect of this new wealth on our society – that while it is mostly, it is not altogether, good. The number of people offering their services as volunteers in community and other social activities has dropped. People are too busy, too stressed, too exhausted to find time. There have been mutterings about breakdown or absence of community, a certain loss of

Irish friendliness, of the Irish welcome afforded to newcomers and visitors. There have been mutterings, some loud, about the fact that by no means does everyone in our society have a fair share in the goods of the new Ireland, that relatively speaking there are people who are worse off now than before. It has been noted that with all the improvement in living standards we are among the most economically unequal societies in Europe, with only the UK, Greece and Portugal being worse than us in this respect. The most recent European Values Study (1999-2000) shows some disturbing attitudes among us to this inequality.[5] There is widespread desire that the basic needs of everyone be met, but this does not get translated into a wish to eliminate inequalities. The same study shows that, while considerably fewer Irish people than heretofore are attending church regularly, we still have a very high percentage who consider themselves religious and who attend church at least monthly. This raises some interesting issues in relation to solidarity and the teaching of the church, and suggests that Catholic social thought on solidarity is probably widely known and feeding into the decisions we are living with. But does this ring true? Or, is the social teaching indeed the Catholic Church's best-kept secret?

Solidarity close to home

One of the striking features of Jon Sobrino's reflection was the fact that, in authentic solidarity, the giver also receives. In thinking about the solidarity or lack of it extended to some of the new communities who have made their home in Ireland, the question of a shared vision arises. Do Irish Christians realise, for example, that a central tenet of Muslim faith shares many aspects of the Christian notion of solidarity and is an example of structural solidarity, which other groups, civic or religious, could well emulate?

The *Zakah* is the third of the five pillars of Islam, without

---

5. European Values Study cited in Tony Fahey, 'Is Atheism Increasing?' in *Measuring Ireland, Discerning Values and Beliefs,* Cassidy ed., Veritas, 2000.

which the faith is incomplete.[6] It is understood as an obligatory act of worship of God, along with praying five times a day, fasting during Ramadan, and making pilgrimage, and is described sometimes as a religious tax. The root of the word signifies purification and it has taken on the sense of almsgiving, but this almsgiving has become quasi official and has been regulated by laws.

Zakah is a kind of tithe meant to support the poor, and those engaged in collecting it, and it has been a factor of solidarity and unity. It is based on the principle that the poor have a right to part of the property of the rich. This principle is stronger than that of a simple appeal to the generosity of those who have. The right of the needy is recognised formally in Qur'an 30, 38. 'Give their right to the near of kin, to the needy, and to the wayfarers.' *Zakah* is constantly mentioned alongside prayer as having been taught by all the prophets before Muhammad. Those who have given also will go to paradise.

The funds can be used to draw people to Islam or to protect the recent faith of others; to buy back slaves who have converted to Islam or Muslims fallen into slavery; to help those overwhelmed with debts to free themselves from their creditors, and for the wayfarer. (Surah 9:60)

For Muslims *Zakah* was an element in the process of re-establishing a new solidarity when the mercantile life of Mecca had broken up the ancient solidarity of the desert. The right to private property remains but the fact that the poor have rights over the property of the rich leads governments to redistribute property in the public interest.

'And in their wealth is the right of the needy and of those deprived of the means of subsistence.' (L1, 19) This Quranic injunction shows that the recipient of charity received it as a matter of right and not as dole.

In Catholic social teaching there is strong emphasis on the

---

6. Thanks to the Islamic Cultural Centre, Clonskeagh, Dublin for several booklets including *Islam: A Brief Guide*, Bleher, 2002, *Towards Understanding Islam*, Mawdudi, 1980.

dignity of the human person and on the notion of the universal destination of the goods of the earth (*Gaudium et Spes*, 1965), but there is something more in the structural solidarity of Islam where sharing, as opposed to charity which is also important in both faiths, is held at the same level as praying. It strikes me that reflecting on the distinction between charity and justice as a fundamental element in the notion of solidarity could well be a good starting point of shared learning, giving and receiving, between interested groups of Muslims and Catholics in Ireland – a means and a method of solidarity. Another area where there is much common ground between the two faiths is ecology. Catholic social thought and Islamic teaching on the right use of the goods of the earth and care and preservation of the environment start from a common base. All is from God, and we are co-creators or vice-regents. Humankind has a responsible and God-given role to play in creation as we hold the earth in trust.[7] Christians and Muslims could find here also a means and method of solidarity with one another and with all life on the earth.

The tsunami disaster has evoked worldwide solidarity and we will need to rely on churches, government and the aid agencies to help us to maintain a committed, ongoing concern that will issue in new mutual understandings and a new kind of giving and receiving between the groups connected by this solidarity. It seems that solidarity in our society, with those very close to home, is much more difficult to build. It may be that the developing ethos of individualism will be challenged by the shock of the realisation that our hold on life is, after all, quite fragile, that we are interdependent and need each other, and that the life of each and every human person in our society is so precious as to warrant the very best care that the group as a whole can provide.

---

7. 'Islam and Ecology', Al-Hafiz B. A. Masri, in *Islam and Ecology*, Ed. Fazlun Khalid with Joanne O'Brien, Cassell, 1992.

CHAPTER TWELVE

The Social Doctrine for a Christian Practice of Liberation

Brendan Mac Partlin SJ

Catholic social teaching uses the term the *social question* to denote the object of its enquiry into the structures of inequality and oppression that have been characteristic of society at national and international levels. It uses the term *the labour question* when it addresses the oppressive aspects of relations between capital and labour. The phenomenon of oppression in society is the reverse side of the process of liberation through which every person aspires to enact the value of freedom. My favourite piece of social teaching that brings these themes together is 'The Social Doctrine of the Church for a Christian Practice of Liberation' which makes up chapter five of the *Instruction on Christian Freedom and Liberation* that was presented at the Vatican in 1986 by none other than Cardinal Ratzinger. For me it throws light on my years of experience as part of the Jesuit effort through the Catholic Workers' College, and its subsequent incarnations, to explore with workers (and managers) issues in the relationship between capital and labour. The issues have taken on new dimensions with the advance of globalisation and with the move of the College to Dublin's new financial district in the Docklands. It is ironic that this new part of Dublin is flowering where dramas of oppression and liberation were enacted in former days.

In this article I will take four of the main themes from the chapter on the Christian Practice of Liberation and relate them to the college's work in the education of workers and in the process to give some account of Catholic social teaching. The first theme deals with Ratzinger's assertion of the right of the poor to education and culture. The college, in its origins, responded to the need of workers, at that time, for education especially in the field of social and economic action. It drew on Catholic social teaching as the medium for education. The second theme gives a vision of the structures of a just society and the principles of freedom and concern that must guide its formation. The college tackled this area under the heading of 'Man and Society'. The third section proposes that work is the key to the transformation of society into a civilisation of freedom and justice and that the lessons we have learned in the struggle over the labour question provide the methods of solidarity that will lead to transformation. The module 'Industrial Society' approached related questions in this area. The fourth theme addresses concerns about unbalanced globalisation and makes proposals for a process of global liberation. The college module on 'Political Philosophy] dealt with questions about the nation state that now have to be reformulated in the context of multinational structures of governance.

I. THE CATHOLIC WORKERS' COLLEGE AND THE RIGHT TO EDUCATION AND CULTURE

In 1947 the Jesuits set up a three man entity called the Catholic Workers' College and bought Sandford Lodge as a step towards meeting the order's directive to do something about social concern. In 1951, after much reflection on social and economic needs the college opened it doors for the education of workers (not excluding managers) who at that time used to leave school at an early age and felt that they needed further development to deal with their duties in a flourishing trade union movement. Ratzingers's account of inequality of access to education could well be applied, in retrospect, to this situation:

> It is a common pattern that rights to education and culture are denied to the less well off in poor economies. The unjust inequalities in the possession and use of material goods are accompanied by similarly unjust inequalities in the opportunity for culture. Every person has a right to culture in view of its being part of a truly human existence. Education, and pri-

marily the elimination of illiteracy, helps greatly to rectify this denial of rights. One gains access to culture through the development of intellectual capacities, moral virtues, abilities to relate to other human beings, and talents for creating things that are useful and beautiful.

He goes on to relate education with the development of a person's freedom, which in turn brings access to culture. A political and social system that respects freedom and participation plays a role in the authentic development of free persons. It is therefore an injustice to keep people marginalised from participation or to limit their freedoms whether through a totalitarian concept of social life or a narrowly economic outlook or on the pretext of the demands of security. To reduce education to an ideology is to turn it into the servant of political or economic power is to debase culture.

It was from this point of view that the Jesuits engaged in education for workers and not, as is sometimes alleged, to indoctrinate workers against communist influence, nor in opposition to The People's College. Both colleges, I would suggest, shared a similar goal in making up for a deficit in working class education. The Jesuits followed a strategy of industrial relations and trade union education while the People's College followed one of providing a wide spectrum of cultural programmes. While their social visions may have differed, both colleges aspired to the liberation of people through educational development and enjoyment of the cultural goods of society. But what is it in education that can promote liberation and unlock access to culture?

The Jesuit approach was to base their education in Catholic social teaching which, far from being a sectarian ideology, is based on a methodology that can act as the basis of a sound pedagogy. Ratzinger's (1986 # 73) text explains succinctly. He proposes that the church's social teaching aims to serve the true good of humanity and to bring about the profound changes demanded by situations of poverty and injustice. It offers a set of

- principles for reflection

- criteria for judgement and
- directives for action

The Jesuit pedagogy was to form their students according these principles of 'see, judge, and act'. There are today elder trade unionists who claim that it was this formation that stood to them in their subsequent activities and they regret its occlusion in the delivery of more informational and technical programmes of today's trade union studies. As forms of basic reasonableness and rationality these principle are implicit in training and educational activities, but it is the ability to use them in a reflexive manner that makes the difference between science and muddling through, or between ethics and pragmatism. They go back to Aristotle and have nothing particularly religious about them that would make them unacceptable to secular projects. Catholic social teaching is based, through these principles, on human science and human wisdom. It deals with action and the ethical aspect of life in society. New questions arise in society and, being open to new questions, it develops with the times. Many of its judgements are therefore contingent and open to review, as is the case with any true science. It has, nevertheless, also developed perennial principles.

To be true to Ratzinger's account there is a religious motivation as to why Christians use their collective heads in this way. They have known the oppression of sin and the experience of liberation through God's unconditional regard. Christ restored their capacity to love and commands them to love their neighbour in justice. The attempt to put this command into practice encounters the problems of life in society and in this encounter is born the social teaching of the church.

II. THE PERSON IN A JUST SOCIETY

The purpose of the Jesuit module, Man and Society, was to explore the nature of the human person and how the collaboration of persons is the origin and consequence of a fair society. The Ratzinger text captures the key concepts in the relationship between the individual and society – individual freedom, society as a co-operative venture, the common good, solidarity and subsidiarity. In summary it argues as follows:

The realisation that we are loved and expected to love leads to a valuing of the human person who is made in God's image. This recognition of the dignity of the person grounds the emergence of natural rights and duties. Central to these is freedom of action. Persons are the active and responsible subjects of social life. They aspire to be free and seek their full development. The category of liberation is a fundamental one and a first principle of action. It seeks to maximise the potential of people, not just as individuals, but also collectively, recognising that the interdependence of all is a necessary condition for the full development of the person.

The principle of solidarity follows from the interdependence that is necessary for integral development. Solidarity captures the notion of the responsibility of all for the good of each and of each for the good of all. It is reasonable that individuals should co-operate to achieve goods that are beyond the capacity of individuals alone. Individuals then draw on the pool of common achievement to enable themselves to develop and realise their potentials. The common good is an outcome of collaborative effort to which each ought to contribute and from which each has a right to draw according to his or her need. Solidarity is a commitment to the common good. It is a more complex idea than individualism yet it offers each individual the potential for greater achievement than an individualist strategy can provide.

Associational life offers various patterns of collaborative effort that aim at different goods. Organisations, teams, states and societies each have as their objective a different common good. In the same way that goods and values can be prioritised and ranked, so too can the array of associations found in society. Freedom of action grounds an ordering of associations. Individuals take responsibility for what they can do for themselves. They enter into association to the extent that they need the co-operation of others to achieve mutually complementary goals. They organise on the basis of a division of labour and of roles and responsibilities. The principle of *subsidiarity* supports the freedom and space of the individual and of intermediary organisations to function at their own level and does not allow the state or society to take this away from them. Statist organisation tends to take freedoms away from people and lesser associations. Individualism does not give enough space to higher levels of co-operative effort. The opposite extremes of statism and individualism tend to undermine intermediary organisation and end up oppressing the individual. A complex grasp of reality guided by the principles of *solidarity* and *subsidiarity* is needed to maintain individual freedom, a thick associational life and a balanced society.

Arguing along these lines the social teaching has developed a set of concepts such as personal dignity, solidarity, subsidiarity, the common good and individual freedom. They are concepts of what is desirable in social organisation. In other words they are values. These values can serve as criteria by which to evaluate social situations, structures and systems. The teaching is particularly concerned about the structures of social life, that is, those patterns of interaction that imprint themselves by repetition as the institutions and practices. They organise and guide the progress of society. They sometimes become fossilised as mechanisms that are relatively independent of the human agent. They can then lose their original meaning and paralyse or distort social development and cause injustice. Structures can facilitate the achievement of social goods but not of themselves apart from the agency of people. Since they originate in human choice they are not necessarily determining and can be changed through free action. It is the quality of the human input that leads to good or flawed outcomes. Therefore the moral integrity of people is an important condition for the health of a society. If economic and social changes are to be really at the service of people then conversion of heart and the priority of freedom are conditions.

The operation of economic, social and political structures and systems can be judged on the extent to which they conform or do not conform to the demands of human dignity. In the end the person, and his/her dignity, is the criterion for systems and structures. If the social situation of many does not meet the demands of constitutionally guaranteed rights, there is no true liberation. A materialist anthroplogy will give priority to structures and technical organisation over the person and the requirements of his dignity. This will bring about situations of injustice that will eventually require far-reaching reforms. In many situations the struggle against injustice aims at establishing a new social and political order. A morality of means would imply a preference for non-violent methods.

In the long history of the labour question, trade unions developed solidaristic action and joint determination as a way preferable to violence. Ratzinger sees the fight of trade unions for the defence of rights, interests and social justice as a reasoned struggle for justice and social solidarity. He learns from this and proposes a similar path of dialogue and joint action as the preferred path for Christians.

III. THE TRANSFORMATION OF SOCIETY

The Jesuit module, Industrial Society, argued, in the words of *Laborem Exercens* (#20), that the nineteenth century brought progress on many fronts but was flawed in so many ways that trade unions emerged as a 'mouthpiece of the struggle for social justice'. Ratzinger analyses 'the modern liberation process' and gives quite a positive interpretation to the history of democracy and, at the same time, points out the ambiguities of the affirmation of freedom. He captures, for example, the logic of how an individualistic ideology that arose under the Enlightenment gave rise to conditions of injustice that in turn gave rise to powerful movements of liberation.

Today, despite the transition to a post-industrial society, or a 'knowledge society', millions of people are caught in an intolerable situation of economic, social and political oppression. The ethical and social heritage of the gospel requires reflection on the relationship between this situation and the commandment of love. The aim of this reflection is to work out programmes aimed at socio-economic liberation and ultimately at bringing about a 'civilisation of love'. The starting point, he claims, is education for a civilisation of work, education for solidarity and access to culture for all. The solution to most of the serious problems related to poverty is to be found in the promotion of a true civilisation of work and, as in *Laborem Exercens*, he sees work as the key to the whole social question.

Work is a fundamental dimension of human existence. People earn their living and survive 'by the sweat of their brow'. The social organisation of work makes it a 'work of our hands' or a 'toil of our bodies'. It is my impression that philosophers before the industrial revolution left unexamined the assumption that necessary work was carried out by the ordinary people whether slaves, domestic workers, agricultural workers or crafts people. It was Marx who brought into focus the centrality of work to human existence. He elaborated on work as an expression of human purposiveness and placed it in the context of the relations of production and the structures of the political economy. He identified ways in which the person was oppressed by structures in the domain of work. Ratzinger adds that the relation between the person and work is so radical and vital that priority must be given to the action of liberation in the domain of work. The forms and models according to which this relationship is regulated will exercise a positive influence for a whole series of social and political problems facing each people. Fair work relationships are a necessary precondition for a system of political community capable of favouring the integral development of every individual.

The great discovery of political science in the field of a people's competitive interest is that 'jaw jaw is better than war war'. The parallel historical insight in the field of labour relations is that 'a talk out is better than a walk out'. Thus the method of collective bargaining became in the 20th century the cornerstone of the relations of production. It could deliver satisfactory resolution to the problems of cost competitiveness and reward, efficiency and participation, job regulation and innovation. It evolved into wider socio-economic systems such as social dialogue and social partnership. In Ireland social partnership has become a voluntary and participative form of socio-economic governance that reconciles the interests of civil society, the market and the state sector and has much to offer as a model in the relations between labour, capital and governance at a global level. Thus Ratzinger proposes that 'if the system of labour relations put into effect by those directly involved succeeds in bringing into existence a civilisation of work, then there will take place a profound and peaceful revolution in people's outlooks and in institutional and political structures' (# 83). He then outlines the values of a civilisation of work:

> A work culture, in a civilisation of work, will recognise the person of the worker as the principle, subject and purpose of work. It will affirm the priority of work over capital. It will hold that material goods are meant for all. It will be animated by a sense of solidarity involving not only rights to be defended but also duties to be performed. It will involve participation, aimed at promoting the national and international common good and not just defending individual or corporate interests. It will assimilate the methods of confrontation and of frank and vigorous dialogue. An outcome will be that the political authorities will become more capable of acting with respect for the legitimate freedoms of individuals, families and subsidiary groups. They will therefore create the conditions necessary for people to be able to achieve their authentic and integral welfare (# 84).

A civilisation of work is also measured by its outcomes. Access for everyone to the goods needed for a worthwhile human, personal and family life is a primary demand of social justice. The poor do not enjoy such equality of access in today's world. The labour question led workers to the discovery of solidarity and methods of non-violent confrontation that brought change to their condition. Ratzinger notes the connection of solidarity with the human and supernatural meanings of brotherhood and sees it as a way of tackling the wider social question of today. New fronts of solidarity, of the poor among themselves, between the poor and the rich, among workers and with workers, are needed for liberation in today's world. Solidarity at all levels of organisation is necessary not only because it is the way to true development but also because world peace depends on it to a great extent.

IV. PROMOTING SOLIDARITY INTERNATIONALLY

The third Jesuit module was Political Philosophy, which addressed the role of the state in the governance of society. It addressed the issues of nations and their governments and economies. Ratzinger suggests that the outstanding problem of global poverty and the great inequality between North and South must lead our thinking beyond the confines of the nation state to address social questions at a global level. He proposes that the concept and practice of solidarity developed by labour in the nineteenth century suggests an approach to the social questions of a globalised world. He offers two principles as guidelines, namely, the principle of brotherhood and the principle that resources are meant for all. These two principles ground the responsibility of richer countries towards developing countries. This responsibility implies: solidarity in aiding developing countries; a revision of the commercial relations between North and South in order to promote social justice; the promotion of a more human world in which each can give and receive without the progress of some being an obstacle to the development of others, nor a pretext for their enslavement.

The issue of inequality between North and South remains crucial today but Ratzinger's account goes no further into an analysis of globalisation. The word was hardly used at the time of his writing. Since that time other disciplines have been calling our attention to a great increase in the deregulation of markets and a liberalisation of the rules governing trade and investment. The search for best return on capital led companies to an international search for the cheaper sourcing of materials and labour.

Developments in transport and logistics enabled them to reach the best markets for their products. New information and communication technologies enabled the movement of finance and outflanked the nation state in controlling its own economic fortunes. The free movement of capital followed the logic of the market. Globalisation progressed in patterns that followed the logic of the market and the interests of the successful players.

Just as the national developments in the nineteenth century were characterised by inequality and injustice, so too are the international developments of the twenty first century. The labour question is expressed in the concern to maintain core labour standards in developing counties. Western countries intent on protecting themselves from the competition of cheap labour, can dress their intentions up as humanitarian concern for the condition of labour in poor countries. The dilemma for the poor country is that there is one situation worse than being exploited and that is not to be exploited when the alternative to child labour can be destitution for the family.

The intensification of competition leads to an intensification of work for workers in the better off countries. Managers, under greater pressure to survive and to keep up the value of their stock quotations, seek to cut costs and get higher productivity through 'high performance management'. In their quest for high performance they individualise their contractual relationship with employees and undermine the solidarity of workers among themselves. They then seek to reconstruct it through teamwork aligned to the company's strategy of competitive advantage.

Technical progress has provided us with the productive capacity to easily meet the world's necessary needs, but the system of market competition condemns many to over work and the rest to under employment. There is unequal distribution of job opportunity as well as an increasingly unequal distribution of earnings per hour worked. Great freedom, well-being and self-fulfilment are enjoyed by some at the expense of greater constraints on the freedoms of others.

Value Change in a Neo Liberal Society

The early sociologists analysed the effects of the market on social life in terms of a trend away from community to individualism. Economic activities that were once embedded in social relations are disembedded by the growth of markets. People living and working in social and economic structures based on market values are being socialised into acting on the belief that the only valid criterion of social usefulness is what the market will bear. Market calculation invades all spheres of society. The logic of the market individualises the lives of people. It encourages self-publicising and assertiveness and discourages an approach to others based on dialogue and respect. The advance of a 'neo-liberal' way of looking at the world leads to an increasing tolerance of inequality.

The free market facilitates the growth of the limited liability company to the extent that business becomes the dominant institution in society and the privatisation of social power weakens all forms of democratic organisation. Market rationality is not a reasonable method of making social progress and this is the case for a globalising society. We need a model of globalisation that humanises life for all people and is sustainable in the longer term. Such a model must surely include a realisation that individual destiny is tied to the fate of humanity and that an inner commitment to well-being of other people is a necessary virtue in the agents of globalisation. They would also be convinced of the need for democratic ways of proceeding. It requires going beyond privatised comfort to engage with others in securing participation. Thus conversion of heart is a pre-requisite condition for virtuous patterns of interaction and good structures.

Political and Democratic Issues

The opening up of international trade has decoupled markets from the nations' social and political controls. The multinational business organisation is able to operate beyond the scope of such control and its hold on social power is increasing while that of the nation state is weakening. It has been a historic achievement for democratic government to centralise social power and direct its use for the common good in a way that is accountable to the citizen. Now, like the nobility of pre-democratic times, business corporations hold the power of mobilising people and resources for their privatised interests and in their decisions have little accountability to others. The development of institutions of political and social control at a global level lags behind the growth of international trade and the corresponding growth in privatised power of corporations. What is needed is the development of democratic power that is transnational and has the capacity to take decisions based on a set of rules that are decided by everyone. It would give priority to collective groups and intergovernmental organisations (e.g. the UN), the NGOs, movements and enterprises in which all social actors can play a role. Institutions would be arranged to meet needs according to the principle of 'subsidiarity'. This would direct decision making and action to the level appropriate to the issue, whether at local or global level. The concept of citizenship would operate in different ways at different levels so that people could identify with their own cultures as well as with regional and global culture. When globalisation is driven by the logic of the market the cultural outcome is split between McDonaldisation and Jihad. When globalisation proceeds along a reasonable, just and solidaristic path a global culture subscribed to by the people of the world is possible.

Conclusion
The liberation of all people from the evils of poverty and oppression is a goal that is not beyond the technical capacity of global society. But the social and political structures for achieving it are lagging far behind. The social teaching on the practice of Christian liberation needs to find again common ground with democratising forces and new movements of solidarity as it has found, in retrospect, with trade unions and working class movements. It has learned form their methods. It also identifies the

role of personal conversion in grounding a commitment to others that evolves the structures and processes necessary for a sustainable path of globalisation.

Where Latin America had its liberation theology and Asian and African countries had inculturation, this piece of social teaching articulates for me, a hitherto missing, liberation ethic for Western liberal democracies and for the world as a whole.

There is however a further dimension of Catholic social teaching that has not been dealt with in this article. It is the dimension of evangelisation and the proclamation of the word out of which Ratzinger proposes the inculturation of gospel values as a process of leavening the dough. Inculturation is an intimate transformation of authentic cultural values by the implantation of the gospel in the different human cultures. If the gospel is faithfully proclaimed the encounter will give fresh life to the cultures of the world. Faith inspires criteria of judgement, determining values, lines of thought and patterns of living that are valid for the whole human community. Social teaching can therefore indicate the lines of a culture in which work is recognised in its full human dimension and in which all would find opportunities for personal self-fulfilment. In devoting herself to this task the church hopes to evoke an immense liberating effort.

References

Messner, J., 1949, *Social Ethics*, St Louis: Herder.

Stiglitz, J., 2002, *Globalization and its Discontents*, Penguin Books.

Dolors Oller I Sala, M., 2004, *A Future for Democracy: A democracy for world governability*, Barcelona: Christianisme I Justicia Booklets.

Ratzinger, Joseph Cardinal, 1986, *Instruction on Christian Freedom and Liberation*, London: Catholic Truth Society.

Dore, Ronald, 2004, 'New forms and meanings of work in an increasingly globalised world', International Institute for Labour Studies: ILO Social Policy Lectures.

John Paul II, 1981, *Laborem Exercens*. London: Catholic Truth Society.

The Contributors

PETER MCVERRY is a Jesuit priest and Director of the Arrupe Society, an organisation working with homeless young people in Dublin. He is author of *The Meaning Is In The Shadows*.

PAUL ANDREWS, a Jesuit priest from Omagh, has worked as a teacher, headmaster, psychologist, psychotherapist, and for the last few years as rector of Manresa retreat house in Dublin. He is the author, among other books, of the best-selling *Changing Children*.

RONAN BARRY works with *Slí Eile* (an Irish Jesuit initiative working with young adults) as coordinator of the *Slí Eile* Volunteer Communities in Ireland. Previously, over a period of ten years, he worked with young people at risk. Ronan is married to Joanne and they have two sons, Tim and Cian.

DAVID BEGG is general Secretary of the Irish Congress of Trade Unions and an Executive Member of the European Trade Union Conference. He is a Director of the Irish Central Bank and chairperson of the Democracy Commission. Previously he was Chief Executive of Concern Worldwide and a Trustee of Trócaire.

MICHAEL BINGHAM is a Jesuit, born in Buckinghamshire and son of a Belfast man. Currently he works in Portadown with community groups and organisations as an Associate Member of Mediation Northern Ireland. He previously spent nine years in Colombia and fourteen years in Liverpool working in Community Development and Pastoral work.

JIM CORKERY is an Irish Jesuit from Limerick now working in Dublin. He teaches theology at the Milltown Institute.

SUSAN JONES is a Holy Faith Sister. She is a graduate of the Milltown Institute. Susan works as a full-time chaplain in St

Wolstan's Community School, Celbridge, Co Kildare and is currently studying for the MA in School Chaplaincy and Pastoral Care at the Mater Dei Institute of Education.

FINOLA KENNEDY is an economist and author of *Cottage to Creche, Family Change in Ireland*. She was a member of the Review Group on the Constitution.

BRENDAN MACPARTLIN is a Jesuit priest from Dublin and lecturer in Employment Relations and Business Ethics at The National College of Ireland. He holds a doctorate from the Business Studies Department of Trinity College and is an active member of a trade union and delegate to the Dublin Council of Trade Unions.

CATHY MOLLOY is a research officer at the Jesuit Centre for Faith and Justice and author of *Marriage: Theology and Reality*.

ANN SCULLY is a Religious Sister of Mercy and was Founder and Director of *DORAS Luimní*, until 2004. She now works at the Justice Desk of the Irish Sisters of Mercy.

DAVID TUOHY is a Jesuit priest, currently working as an independent consultant in education. He has a particular interest in school and teacher development, especially in clarifying the Catholic character of the school. He has written extensively and has lectured in England, the US and Australia, as well as evaluating education provision for refugees in East Africa.

GERARD WHELAN is an Irish Jesuit based in Kenya and a member of the East African Province of the Jesuits. He is parish priest in a slum parish in Nairobi where he also teaches pastoral theology at the Jesuit School of Theology in the city. Among other works, he is involved in representing the Holy See to the United Nations organisation for shelter UN-Habitat.